ARCHIPELAGO

Antonella Anedda is a poet and essayist who lives in Rome, and presently works as a lecturer in Lugano. She has published five collections of poetry, which have won many prizes including the Premio Sinisgalli for a first collection, the International Montale Prize, the Dessì Prize, the Napoli Prize, and her most recent book was given, among other awards, the prestigious Premio Viarreggio-Repaci. She has translated Sappho and Ovid from the classics as well as numerous recent poets including Philippe Jaccottet and Anne Carson. The four books of essays which she has published are principally concerned with literature and the visual arts, though her last prose work *Isolatria* was a study of Sardinia.

Though born in Rome (in 1955), she comes from a Sardinian family and has passed a great deal of her life between the capital and a small island, La Maddalena, off the coast of Sardinia, which has continued to deeply inform both her poetry and her prose. Her work has been translated into many European languages as well as into Japanese, Korean and Hebrew. Her first English edition, *Archipelago*, translated by Jamie McKendrick, was published by Bloodaxe Books in 2014.

Jamie McKendrick, born in Liverpool, 1955, is a poet and translator. His translations include the anthology *The Faber Book of Italian 20th-Century Poems*, which he edited; *The Embrace: Selected Poems by Valerio Magrelli* (Faber, 2009), which was awarded the John Florio Prize and the Oxford-Weidenfeld Prize for translation; the bilingual edition *Archipelago* by Antonella Anedda (Bloodaxe Books, 2014); a verse play by Pier Paolo Pasolini, *Fabrication* (Oberon, 2010); two novels by Giorgio Bassani, *The Garden of the Finzi-Continis* and *The Gold-Rimmed Spectacles* and the short stories *The Smell of Hay*, published by Penguin Classics. His own books of poetry include *The Marble Fly* (1997), which won the Forward Prize, *Sky Nails: Poems 1979-1997* (2000), *Ink Stone* (2003), *Crocodiles & Obelisks* (2007), and most recently *Out There* (2012), which won the Hawthornden Prize.

Archipelago

ANTONELLA ANEDDA

translated by

JAMIE McKENDRICK

BLOODAXE BOOKS

ISBN: 978 1 78037 108 5

First published 2014 by
Bloodaxe Books Ltd,
Eastburn,
South Park,
Hexham,
Northumberland NE46 1BS.

www.bloodaxebooks.com
For further information about Bloodaxe titles
please visit our website or write to
the above address for a catalogue.

Supported using public funding by
**ARTS COUNCIL
ENGLAND**

This book has been selected to receive financial assistance from English PEN's
'PEN Translates!' programme, supported by Arts Council England (see page 160).
This book has been translated thanks to a translation grant awarded by the Italian
Ministry for Foreign Affairs. *Questo libro e' stato tradotto grazie ad un contributo
alla traduzione assegnato dal Ministero degli Affari Esteri Italiano.*

Cover design: Neil Astley & Pamela Robertson-Pearce.

Printed in Great Britain by Bell & Bain Limited, Glasgow, Scotland, on
acid-free paper sourced from mills with FSC chain of custody certification.

CONTENTS

9   INTRODUCTION

15   A NOTE ON THE TRANSLATION AND SELECTION

FROM *Residenze invernali* | **Winter Residences** 1992

18   I *Le nostre anime dovrebbero dormire...*

19   I Our souls should sleep...

22   II *Sui vetri appannati dal freddo passavano ombre confuse...*

23   II Confused shadows crossed the window-panes...

26   III *Prima di cena, prima che le lampade scaldino i letti...*

27   III Before supper, before the lamp warms the beds...

28   DA *Chiusa di vento*

29   FROM Wind Lock

FROM *Notti di pace occidentale* | **Nights of Western Peace** 1999

34   I *Vedo dal buio...*

35   I I see from the darkness...

36   II *Non volevo nomi per morti sconosciuti...*

37   II I didn't want to name the unknown dead...

38   III *Per trovare la ragione di un verbo...*

39   III To discover the reason for a verb...

40   IV *Correva verso un rifugio, si proteggeva la testa...*

41   IV She was running towards a refuge, covering her head...

42   VI *Non esiste innocenza in questa lingua...*

43   VI This language has no innocence...

44   VII *Forse se moriamo è per questo?...*

45   VII If we die, perhaps it's for this?...

46   XIII *Anche questi sono versi di guerra...*

47   XIII These too are war poems...

48   *a mia figlia*

49   to my daughter

50   *Se ho scritto è per pensiero...*

51   If I've written it's for thought...

52   *Volevo che il mio amore non finisse...*

53   I wanted my love not to end...

54   *nella morte di Amelia Rosselli*
55   at the death of Amelia Rosselli

FROM *Il catalogo della gioia* | **Catalogue of Joy** 2003

60   *Aprile, La Maddalena. Resti di sogni*
61   April, La Maddalena Island. Dream Fragments
62   *Maggio, La Maddalena. Resti di sogni*
63   May, La Maddalena Island. Dream Fragments
64   *Settembre 2001. Arcipelago della Maddalena, isola di S. Stefano*
65   September 2001, Maddalena Archipelago, Island of S. Stefano
66   *Una terra*
67   Earth
68   *f*
69   f
68   *i*
69   i
70   *Arcipelago (un collasso)*
71   Archipelago (heart failure)
72   *Coraggio*
73   Courage
74   *Silenzio notturno...*
75   Night silence...

FROM *Dal balcone del corpo* | **From the Body's Balcony** 2007

78   *Contro Scaurum* †
79   Against Scaurus
80   *Limba* †
81   Tongue
82   *Attittos* †
83   Dirges
84   *Tra il prima e il poi. Incidente*
85   Between Now and Then: Accident
88   *Così arrivono i delitti*
89   In This Way Crimes Come About

† *indicates poems in Logudorese*

90   *Coro*
91   Chorus
92   *Amore e corvo*
93   Love and the Crow
94   *Coro*
95   Chorus
96   *All'angelo, dopo la cacciata*
97   To the Angel, after the Expulsion
98   *Coro*
99   Chorus
100 *Getsemani*
101 Gethsemane
102 *Cana*
103 Cana
104 *Coro*
105 Chorus
106 *Anestesie*
107 Anaesthetics

FROM *La vita dei dettagli* | The Life of Details 2009

110 *Sono i piedi di un morto…*
111 They are a dead man's feet… [MANTEGNA]
112 *Dimmi a chi appartiene questa casa…*
113 Tell me whose house this is… [BOSCH]
114 *Hendrickje Stoffels solleva la camicia…*
115 Hendrickje Stoffels lifts her chemise [REMBRANDT]
116 *Di chi sono questi occhi…*
117 Whose are these eyes… [GÉRICAULT]
118 *Pensa la fame, pensa la sete…*
119 He thought of hunger, thought of thirst… [GÉRICAULT]
120 *Figlio di un barbiere, nipote di un macellaio…*
121 Barber's son, butcher's nephew… [TURNER]
122 *Cespugli cespugli cespugli…*
123 Bushes bushes bushes… [SEGANTINI]
124 *Vivendo di sogni, percorrendo le strade…*
125 Living off dreams, wandering the streets… [CORNELL]

FROM *Salva con nome* | Save As 2012

128   *Cucina*

129   Kitchen

130   *Casa-madre*

131   Mother House

132   *Spazio dell'invecchiare*

133   Space to Grow Old in

134   *Malas mutas* †

135   Bad Tidings

136   *8-8.*

137   8/8

138   *Ritratto di tuffatrice*

139   Portrait of a Woman Diving

140   *Aquedotto*

141   Aqueduct

142   *Cucire*

143   Sewing

144   *Un giorno ho pensato che ci sarebbe voluto tempo...*

145   One day I thought there would still be time...

146   *Se devo scrivere poesie ora che invecchio...*

147   If I must write now I'm growing old...

148   *Non riesco a sentirti, sta passando un camion...*

149   I can't hear you – a lorry laden with iron...

150   *Spettri*

151   Ghosts

152   *Mattino 7:00–12:00*

153   Morning 7.00–12.00

154   *Non ti ho detto che la mia paura...*

155   I didn't tell you that my fear...

156   *Lezione*

157   Lesson

158   *Lo spirito – dice Eckhart – è una montagna di piombo...*

159   The spirit – according to Eckhart – is a mountain of lead...

160   ACKNOWLEDGEMENTS

INTRODUCTION

'One must have a mind of winter' begins Wallace Stevens's 'The Snow Man'. Antonella Anedda in her first book of poems would seem to have taken this perspective to heart, along with its final stanza:

> For the listener, who listens in the snow,
> And, nothing himself, beholds
> Nothing that is not there and the nothing that is.

Its title *Residenze invernali* (Winter Residences, 1992), could hardly strike a less Italian note – and in fact these dwellings appear to be sited mostly in some northern zone, a St Petersburg of the soul, as though Tsarskoye Selo has been crossed with an ancient, dilapidated hospital in Rome. They are dream interiors – dream bordering on nightmare – and at the same time they have the frosty clarity of Joseph Cornell's 'Setting for a Fairy Tale', a detail from which she would later use in her prose book *La vita dei dettagli*. The inmates or patients of these imagined hospital wards are ailing or dying, deprived almost of movement or communication though they may 'signal as from distant boats' to each other.

Not only is the weather inclement and un-Mediterranean, but the spiritual atmosphere is senescent, reduced and bitten back to the core. It's a curious debut for a poet not yet 30 years old. It has more affinities with Anna Akhmatova and Osip Mandelstam, perhaps even with Marina Tsvetaeva, than with the Italian lyrical tradition, even that lineage of poets like Franco Fortini and Amelia Rosselli who, following Montale, have sought to challenge it. The Russian Acmeists are not so much a direct influence as an example – and the same could be said of Philippe Jaccottet, whose collection *La Semaison* (mixing prose and poetry) she translated into Italian. The opening of one of his prose pieces – 'L'attachement à soi augmente l'opacité de la vie' – sounds a warning note that will recur in her own poems.

If the perspective of Anedda's first book of poems was Eastern European, the title of her second, *Notti di pace occidentale* (1999), signals an apparent move westward though it retains the sense of an outsider's, even a foreigner's view. The poems were written in the wake of the first Gulf War and of the break up of the former Yugoslavia – the latter a war very close to Italy's borders and involving territories such as Slovenia with an intimate connection to Italy, and so the 'Western peace' it speaks of carries a bitter irony and a distinct uneasiness. As she writes in an afterword: 'The idea that lingers in the title is that of the West surrounded by apparently concluded wars and of a Europe which is not living in peace but in a frightened truce.' 'La tregua' (the title of Primo Levi's sequel to *If This Is a Man*) is a recurrent word in Anedda's lexicon – sometimes literally a truce, sometimes meaning a space for repose, or more idiomatically a relief) and the eponymous section first appeared under the title 'Versi per una tregua'. Is this a peace only maintained by exporting war to other places? A delusion or a deception? All of these questions are in play throughout the book, which has a decisive, if exhausted, tone of civic and ethical engagement.

As I've begun by considering the titles of Anedda's first two books, it may be helpful to offer some notes of a similar kind on the succeeding three volumes to date. *Il catalogo della gioia* (Catalogue of Joy, 2003), Anedda's third collection, again presents an ambiguous title, but its references to the Zohar and its epigraph from the Hasidic Rabbi Nachman of Breslov ('To someone who asked him what difference there was between being sad and having a broken heart, Nachman replied that to have a broken heart was not an impediment to joy') strongly suggests a movement towards a poetics which might counter the bleaker landscapes that preceded it. The concluding sequence on La Maddalena, an island off Sardinia, puts this island perspective further into the foreground of her poetry; dream, memory and reality are all reconfigured in this archipelagic setting.

The title of her fourth volume, *Dal balcone del corpo* (From the Body's Balcony, 2007), may be recalling her own earlier poem from *Notti di pace occidentale*: 'I see from the darkness / as from the most radiant balcony', but the image in both cases recalls Baudelaire's famous sonnet 'Recueillement' with its self-estranged and paradoxical consideration of suffering: 'Sois sage, ô ma Douleur, et tiens-toi plus tranquille', and more particularly its architecture of the psyche: 'Vois se pencher les défuntes Années, / Sur les balcons du ciel, en robes surannée' – in Robert Lowell's translation: 'Look, the dead years dressed / in old clothes crowd the balconies of the sky' (though that misses the slightly sinister or perilous way the years lean out over the sky's balconies). The book's initial working title was *Cori* (Choruses) – there are a number of poems simply entitled 'Coro' – and perhaps here more than before in Anedda's work, as from a balcony, we hear the voices and the lives of others. Although some critics saw the title as indicating a feminist slant to the work, Anedda in an interview has remarked that she hadn't considered this body as having a specific gender, but that, in reference to a statement by Husserl, all of us 'lean out from our own body as from a balcony, attached to an interior yet suspended above something, unable properly to turn around'.

Salva con nome (2012), her fifth volume, has yet another ambiguous title. The phrase corresponds, as a computer direction, to the English 'Save As' but may also be read as an imperative (second person singular) 'save with the name' as well as a third person indicative 'he/she saves by naming'. The book opens with the prose poem 'Il Componidori' (a figure in a Sardinian festival who sheds his actual name and gender) and ends with a visual collage composed of pieces of anonymous faces. The visual element of photographs and images which accompany the poems has been excluded from the translation for reasons of space and to give priority to the poems themselves, but it is undeniably a striking component of the original book.

* * *

The ambivalence that I noted Anedda has towards the Italian lyric tradition – rich and various as it undoubtedly is – has become, if anything, more marked with each new collection. It is a kind of temperamental opposition – even to the language itself. Her own language, effortlessly musical, throws obstacles and calthrops in its course, and gives space to quotidian things such as pots, pans, cutlery, needles. Such imagery might be considered feminine or domestic, but her handling of it tends to emphasise the metallic, angular and obdurate qualities of these objects, their *Dinglichkeit* or thingish quiddity, and a kitchen rather than offering an image of domestic peace is as likely to be the site of a haunting – see her poem 'Cucina' (Kitchen).

One immediately notable feature of her writing from the outset is how her poems can stray into prose, and return, or start in prose and turn to poetry, breaking the line, breaking with the line, then reconstructing it. Many years later, she would also break with the language, and her last two collections both include poems written in Logudorese, a language of central Sardinia. The languages she was brought up hearing, apart from Italian, were Logudorese, Catalan from Alghero, and Corsican French mixed with the dialect of la Maddalena. Best here to have her own account of this linguistic sidestep or re-rooting:

It began after an operation… I can only say that at a certain time the sounds that rose in my memory were those harsh ones of a pre-scholastic language, thick with consonants and shorn of adjectives. And I understood my own Italian in the light of those sounds. When I translated these poems from Sardinian into Italian I saw that one language steered or guided the other and that most likely I had always "translated" into Italian from that language.

She adds that the experience involved a descent into 'una lingua non bassa, ma profonda' (a language that isn't low, or vernacular, but deep) such as the writer Luigi Meneghello speaks of.

I think that for the reader too these new poems in Logudorese shed light on her earlier poems in Italian. From her first book with its insistently Russian atmosphere, a sense of otherness and estrangement has always been audible in her poetry, which has a slow, resistant compactness of phrasing. The new poems in Sardinian suggest that those qualities may also involve an encounter between two distinct languages and cultures.

The significance of Sardinia in the mental and actual landscape of this Roman-born poet is worth dwelling on. Sardinia and Rome are poles of her imagination, both geographical and historical. Had dialect per se attracted her, *romanesco* might have been the more obvious, the more local choice. It also has a rich literary history from Belli's satirical and brilliant sonnets to Pasolini's novels and stories from the Roman *borgate*. But Logudorese, with its harsh, consonantal acoustics, of all the languages of Italy (Albanian apart) stands perhaps at the greatest distance from Tuscan Italian – it is called 'limba' (*lingua*: language not dialect even if that distinction is dubious at best) – and also, arguably, at the greatest distance in terms of culture. The depth of that schism can be heard in her poem 'Contro Scauro' ('Against Scaurus'), which decribes how the island's inhabitants were held in contempt by the Imperium, and their plea for justice was dismissed by the Roman orator Cicero: 'A truthless people...land where even the honey is gall.' Incidentally in the original Logudorese, as in Italian, the pun on 'Cicerone', identical for the orator's name and the term for a tourist guide, has been sacrificed in my version, although of course it could have been heard, somewhat mangled by English, if I'd kept Cicero/cicerone. Instead the orator has been transmogrified into a lizard among the ruins.

Even if Sardinia is remote from the mainland of Italy, the most visited site of her poems is a small island at a remove from the island itself. The archipelago of the title, and which many of her poems refer to is La Maddalena, a chain of islands off the north-east coast of Sardinia, in the wind-scoured Straits of Bonifacio stretching out towards Corsica. Her most recent prose book *Isolatria* (2013) offers a revealing backdrop to the poems, with its acute and original mixture of travel writing and spiritual biography, of meteorology and meditation. The 'continente', as the mainland is called by Italian islanders, works as a kind of oppositional field of force to the weather, history and landscape of the island itself.

'September 2001, Maddalena Archipelago, Island of S. Stefano' begins:

> This small island riven underwater by U.S. submarines,
> where my great-grandfather planted citrus fruits and vines,
> built cowsheds and brought ten cows from the mainland...

The poem, set just over the threshold of the new millennium, but overshadowed by historic images of uprooting and undermining, is one example of the way her imagination seizes on this mainland/ island polarity. However important such tensions are within her poems, to make Anedda a poet merely of conflicting local allegiances would be to oversimplify and trammel the force of her writing. In the same interview I mentioned, she gives the Greek etymology of the word 'ethos' as a space ('a habitual gathering place' as I've elsewhere seen it defined) preceeding its later sense of mores and disposition. What's most unusual in her work is a severe distance of perspective and an abrupt, often seering intimacy of tone. Her poems, with their emphasis on space as much as place, are poems of solitude, though they occupy a site curiously equidistant from the self and from the world, the self and others. A place of gathering, an ethical space.

JAMIE McKENDRICK

A Note on the Translation and Selection

Another recurring and emphatic feature of Anedda's poetry from
the outset has been the formal choice of the sequence. Some
sequences are titled as such, whereas others like the poems
concerning sewing in *Salva con nome* are less explicitly signalled
but nevertheless clearly associated. As a reader as well as a
translator of her work I can see the self-sufficiency of many of the
poems that comprise the sequences, but their way of developing a
theme, of carrying it across time and distance is an integral element
of the composition which I've tried at least to suggest. To take two
indicative examples, the title sequence of the first book consists of
seven poems of which I have translated only the first three, and
the title sequence of *Notti di pace occidentale* consists of sixteen
poems, seven of which I have translated. My attempt has been to
offer translations of the poems I've felt best equipped to deal with,
in the hope that selection will not do violence to the entire shape
of the poem but rather allow its contours to emerge. I realise that
there are risks involved here, and feel the reader should be warned.
What this marked tendency undoubtedly signals is the poet's own
reluctance to settle for the one-off, if you like, definitive lyric (how-
ever much, in practice, I'd argue that she also manages to achieve
this). The sequence of often short lyrics has a way of being stations
along an axis in which a single perspective is susceptible to revision
and refraction, and it also suggests an attitude towards the poem
as process, as something continuous and continuing rather than
conclusive. I stress this element in her poetry because in a selection
such as this it can only be partially suggested, and the same goes
for the architecture of each of the five volumes, their careful ordering
of sequences and individual poems which inevitably any selection
distorts.

The visual arts have played a crucial role in Anedda's formation
as a poet. She graduated in Art History at Rome's Sapienza Uni-
versity and over many years has written reviews, articles and essays

on the visual arts. Her experimental prose work *La vita dei dettagli* (2009), is a meditation on the way specific chosen details of works of art (as well as poems) can be recomposed and recontextualised and re-imagined. From this book, I have chosen eight examples which consider details taken from paintings – starting with Mantegna and ending with Cornell. They have been wrested from their context and from the illustrations that accompany them, and are here presented as free-standing prose poems. Beneath each one I have given the titles of the paintings and the names of the painters which Anedda had purposefully kept apart until the end of the chapter. They have become themselves cut and collaged details of details, and while the procedure may seem presumptuous and eccentric, I hope it pays tribute to her own practice in that book, and might offer the reader a telling glimpse of other crucial aspects of her work.

A final note on the translation. I remarked earlier on Anedda's fluctuations between prose and poetry in which the two forms, the lineated and unlineated, are in an unusually close and problematic, even volatile, relation. The effect is more like a seismic than a formal shift. In translating these I've always maintained the form, and observed the demarcation. However, the prose poem 'Non riesco a sentirti, sta passando un camion' ('I can't hear you – a lorry laden with iron') stands as a solitary exception in which the original's prose form has been translated into verse. The only excuse, though a strong one, that I can offer for this deviation is that it just seemed naturally to fall into lines in English, and worked better in that form than in a more accurate prose rendering. In my effort to translate the poem, the percussive sonorities of the original became more audible in lines. The irony of this choice is that one traditional mode of translation has customarily been in the opposite direction: to turn poetry into prose. There are times in translating poetry when, besieged by difficulties, it can make more sense to go *contre sens*.

[JMcK]

Residenze invernale
Winter residences

1992

I

Le nostre anime dovrebbero dormire
come dormono i corpi sottili
stare tra le lenzuole come un foglio
i capelli dietro le orecchie
le orecchie aperte
capaci di ascoltare. Carne
appuntita e fragile, cava
nel buio della stanza. Osso lieve.
Così la membrana stringe
la piuma alla spalla dell'Angelo.

Trasparenti sono le orecchie dei malati
dello stesso colore dei vetri
eppure ugualmente sentono
il rullio dei letti
spostati dalle braccia dei vivi.
Alle quattro, nei giorni di festa
hanno fine le visite. Lentamente
le fronti si voltano verso le pareti.
Nei corridoi vuoti scende una pace d'acquario.
Luci azzure in alto e in basso
sulla cima delle porte
sul bordo degli scalini.

Luci notturne.
I malati dormono gli uni
vicini agli altri posati
su letti uguali.
Solo diverso è il modo
di piegare le ginocchia
se le ginocchia
possono piegare, diversa
l'onda delle loro coperte.

I

Our souls should sleep
as subtle bodies do,
lying between the sheets like a leaf,
hair behind the ears,
ears open and quite
able to hear. Flesh
thinned and frail, hollow
in the ward's darkness. Light bone.
The way fine membrane contracts
round a feather on the Angel's shoulder.

The ears of the sick are transparent,
the same colour as the window panes
and yet, undeterred, they hear
the rolling of beds
pushed by the arms of the living.
At four o'clock on festival days
visits come to an end. Slowly foreheads turn to the walls.
In empty corridors an aquarium peace descends.
Blue lights above and below,
on the tops of doors,
the edge of stairs.

Night lights.
The sick sleep one beside
the other laid out
on identical beds.
The only difference being the way
the knees bend, if their knees
can bend, or the wave
shape their covers make.

Pochi riescono ad alzarsi sulla schiena
come nelle malattie in casa
e ogni letto ha grandi ruote di metallo dentato
molle che di scatto
serrano il materasso
o di colpo lo innalzano.
Il letto stride, si placa.

Luci di Natale.
La corsia è una pianura con impercettibili tumuli.
Con quali silenziosi inchini s'incontrano i pensieri dei morti.

Luci d'inverno.
Nella sala degli infermieri luccicano carte di stagnola
l'odore del vino sale nell'aria.
Se i vivi accostassero il viso ai vetri appannati
se allungassero appena le lingue
il vapore saprebbe di vino.
C'è un attimo prima della morte
la notte gira come una chiave.
Quali misteriosi cenni fanno i lampioni ai moribondi,
quante ombre lasciano i corpi.

Le dieci. Sulla tovaglia un coniglio rovesciato di fianco
patate bollite, asparagi passati in casseruola.
Nella stanza regna una solenne miseria.

I vivi si chiamano come da barche lontane.

Few manage to raise themselves in bed
same as if they'd been at home
and every bed has big wheels of soft
knurled metal which suddenly
lock down a mattress
or raise it up.
The bed creaks, then is lulled.

Christmas lights.
The aisle is a plain with imperceptible mounds.
With what silent bows do the thoughts of the dead meet there.

Winter lights.
In the nurses' room silver foil shines,
the smell of wine wafts in the air.
If the living were to press their faces to the steamed-up windows,
if they could just extend their tongues a little,
the vapour would taste of wine.
There's a moment before death
when the night turns like a key.
What strange signals the lamps make to the dying,
how many shadows their bodies cast.

Ten o'clock. On the tablecloth a rabbit turned on its side,
boiled potatoes, overcooked asparagus in a pan.
A solemn poverty reigns on the ward.

The living call to each other as from distant boats.

II

Sui vetri appannati dal freddo passavano ombre confuse. Nel
cielo, oltre le case, salivano fuochi d'artificio. Quando le lancette
degli orologi raggiunsero le dodici, da uno dei letti vicino alla
finestra venne una breve risata infelice.

È scesa una notte orientale, si è incollata sui tetti.
Di colpo come nei presepi
da una fessura del cielo è precipitata la neve.
Davanti alla sponda del letto sfilavano silenziose le renne
contro il legno degli armadi ardevano i fuochi dei lapponi
fuori crepitavano rami e bottiglie
bruciavano alberi di natale:
legno e vetro, segreto scintillio di carte.

È arrivato il Capodanno.
Noi abbiamo vegliato senza fatica, semplicemente
la luna spezzava le travi, l'ombra di una calza velava il cortile,
ogni lume era spento.

Gennaio lascia nelle isole
gusci di riccio sugli scogli
e tesa luce sulle secche invernali.
Come una desolata corona di pietra
in un naufragio polare
lastre di granito e chiuse lapidi
nell'acqua e in terra
oltre il promontorio della Trinità
dentro il recinto del cimitero.

Vi chiedo coraggio: sognate con la dignità degli esuli
e non con il rancore dei malati
cancellando la visione dei muri e della neve

II

Confused shadows crossed the window-panes the cold had steamed
up. Beyond the houses, fireworks climbed the sky. When the clock
hands reached twelve, from one of the beds near the window
came a short unhappy laugh.

An oriental night has fallen. It has stuck to the roofs.
Suddenly as in nativity scenes
from a crack in the sky snow fell.
Reindeer filed silently past the bedside.
Lappish fires flamed against the wooden wardrobes.
Outside branches and bottles cracked;
Christmas trees burned:
wood and glass, the secret gleam of wrapping paper.

New Year has come.
We have kept vigil without effort, simply.
The moon split the wooden beams, the shadow of a stocking
veiled the courtyard. All the lights were out.

January deposits sea-urchin shells among the islands,
on the rocks, and a tense light
is stranded on the winter sandbanks.
Like a desolate crown of stone
in an arctic shipwreck,
slabs of granite and headstones
lie in the water and on the earth,
beyond Trinity headland
within the cemetery's precinct.

I ask you for courage: you should dream with the dignity
of exiles, not the rancour of the sick,
cancelling the vision of walls and snow,

trasformando l'ombra sporca dei fiocchi e la sagoma scura dei
     gabbiani
con l'animo teso dei marinai
che ammutoliscono al sollevarsi dell'onda
e pregano
raccolti nel cesto del vento.

Un filo d'acqua scende nel lavabo.
Il ghiaccio riga le finestre
ed è difficile pensare al soffio marino
e l'urtare dei carrelli
e il fischio di sirena mattutino
non contemplano nessun eroismo.
Eppure, distesi sulla misteriosa rotta dei letti
noi siamo nello stesso splendore
della marea che si placa, vicinissimi al nodo che l'acqua finalmente
     distende.

La nave salpa e cammina
ed è un quieto santuario.

and altering the soiled shadow of the snowflakes and the gulls'
        dark form
with the tense soul of seafarers
who hush at the waves rising
and pray
gathered up in the chest of the winds.

A thread of water falls in the washstand.
Ice encrusts the windows
and it's hard to think of the sea breeze:
the collision of serving-trolleys
and the whistle of the dawn siren
have nothing heroic about them.
Yet, stretched on the beds' mysterious sea lane,
we are wrapped in the same splendour
as the tide which grows becalmed
right up close to that knot the water finally unties.

The ship weighs anchor, sets sail
and is a quiet sanctuary.

III

Prima di cena, prima che le lampade scaldino i letti e il fogliame degli alberi sia verde-buio e la notte deserta. Nel breve spazio del crepuscolo passano intere sconosciute stagioni; allora il cielo si carica di nubi, di correnti che sollevano ceppi e rovi. Contro i vetri della finestra batte l'ombra di una misteriosa bufera. L'acqua rovescia i cespugli, le bestie barcollano sulle foglie bagnate. L'ombra dei pini si abbatte sui pavimenti; l'acqua è gelata, di foresta: Il tempo sosta, dilegua. Di colpo, nella quiete solenne dei viali, nel vuoto delle fontane, nei padiglioni illuminati per tutta la notte, l'ospedale ha lo sfolgorio di una pietroburghese residenza invernale.

Ci sarà un incubo peggiore
socchiuso tra i fogli dei giorni
non sbatterà nessuna porta
e i chiodi
piantati all'inizio della vita
si piegheranno appena.
Ci sarà un assassino disteso sul ballatoio
il viso tra le lenzuola, l'arma posata di lato.
Lentamente si schiuderà la cucina
senza fragore di vetri infranti, nel silenzio del pomeriggio invernale.
Non sarà l'amarezza, né il rancore, solo
per un attimo le stoviglie
si faranno immense di splendore marino.

Allora occorrerà avvicinarsi, forse salire
là dove il futuro si restringe
alla mensola fitta di vasi
all'aria rovesciata del cortile
al volo senza slargo dell'oca,
con la malinconia del pattinatore notturno che a un tratto conosce
il verso del corpo e del ghiaccio
voltarsi appena,
andare

III

Before supper, before the lamps warm the beds and the trees'
foliage absorbs the dark and the night's abandoned. In the curtailed
space of dusk whole seasons pass by unrecognised. Then the sky's
freighted with clouds and air-currents drum at brambles and stumps.
A storm shadow beats against the window panes. Water ruffles the
shrubs and the animals stagger over drenched leaves. Pine shadows
fall on the paving stones; the water's frozen – forest water. Time
halts, disperses. Suddenly in the solemn quiet of the avenues, in the
hollow fountains, in the pavilions lit up all night, the hospital has
the blaze of a St Petersburg winter residence.

There'll be a worse nightmare
half-closed between the calendar's sheets
which will slam no door and the nails
hammered home when life began
will hardly bend.
There'll be an assassin stretched out in the gallery,
his face between the sheets, the weapon at one side.
Slowly the kitchen will open itself up
without the crash of broken glass
in the silence of a winter afternoon.
There'll be no bile or bitterness, just
– for one moment – the crockery
will loom with a marine splendour.

Then will be the time to draw near, perhaps to climb up
there where the future narrows
to a shelf packed with jars,
to the capsized air of the courtyard,
to the cramped flight of the goose
with the melancholy of a night skater
who suddenly knows
how the body aligns itself with the ice
so as to turn away
and go.

da Chiusa di vento

Pensa gli strumenti per la casa
il martello nell'ombra del ripostiglio
i chiodi sparsi sul panno, la sega
il traforo gelato del cesto.
Hanno spento fuoco e lampioni
hanno chiuso le persiane di legno
ogni stanza conosce soltanto
una riga di luna invernale.
Velati divani e sedie
rovesciati una bottiglia e un bicchiere
dissolte le sale
nella bruma dei lenzuoli e di buio.

Con cura l'inverno prepara la sua sventura
con mesta ossessione accatasta luce su neve
ad uno ad uno ammaestra gli uccelli
nel freddo dei fili e dei rami, nei letti di sola rete
nell'onda dei materassi
lasciati a sfioccare col vento.
Nulla offusca la casta bellezza di questa miseria
il tizzone brucia in un camino lontano
l'acqua si raccoglie altrove
in conche di quiete domestica, in case lucenti
dai viali al portone.
L'inverno dispone il suo tempo
come pane lo posa sui davanzali di pietra
con calma raccoglie il mio sguardo
il tuo collo il geranio forato dal passero
la carta che la pioggia ha bagnato.

from Wind Lock

Think of the house's implements:
the hammer in the lumber-room's shadow,
the nails scattered on the cloth, the saw,
the basket's chill filigree.
They have put out the fire and turned off the lights,
closed the wooden shutters
so the floors witness no more than
a stripe of winter moonlight.
Covered sofas and chairs,
a bottle on its side next to an upturned glass,
the rooms dissolved
in the fog of sheets and dark.

With care winter prepares its misfortunes,
with gloomy obsessiveness heaps light on snow,
schools the birds one by one
in the cold of wires and branches, reveals the bare bed frames,
the wave shapes of the mattresses
left to air in the wind.
Nothing darkens this chaste and wretched beauty.
The spill burns in a far-off fireplace,
elsewhere water gathers
in bowls of domestic quiet, in houses that light
driveways up to the doorstep.
Winter casts its time
like bread on stone sills,
calmly gathers my gaze, the curve
of your neck, the sparrow-pecked geranium,
rain-soaked paper.

La chiave dondola nel gesto notturno.
Conta i passi, conta le scaglie di trave tra le scarpe.
Andremo a lungo adesso
corpo accanto a corpo
nel breve spazio che ci hanno assegnato.
Ancora capaci di gettare ombre sui muri
ancora mortali.

The key swings back and forth in a nocturnal rite.
Count the steps, count the floorboard splinters underfoot.
From now there's time enough for us to go
on, one beside the other,
in the brief space given to us.
Still able to cast shadows
on the wall, still mortal.

Notti di pace occidentale
Nights of Western Peace
1999

I

Vedo dal buio
come dal più radioso dei balconi.
Il corpo è la scure: si abbatte sulla luce
scostandola in silenzio
fino al varco più nudo – al nero
di un tempo che compone
nello spazio battuto dai miei piedi
una terra lentissima
– promessa –

I

I see from the darkness
as from the most radiant balcony.
The body is an axe: it strikes the light
silently removing it
to its starkest passage – to the black
of a time that composes
from the space trodden down by my soles
an unbearably slow
promised land.

II

Non volevo nomi per morti sconosciuti
eppure volevo che esistessero
volevo che una lingua anonima
– la mia –
parlasse di molte morti anonime.
Ciò che chiamiamo pace
ha solo il breve sollievo della tregua.
Se nome è anche raggiungere se stessi
nessuno di questi morti ha raggiunto il suo destino.

Non ci sono che luoghi, quelli di un'isola
da cui scrutare il Continente
l'oriente – le sue guerre
la polvere che gettano a confondere
il verdetto: noi non siamo salvi
noi non salviamo
se non con un coraggio obliquo
con un gesto
di minima luce.

II

I didn't want to name the unknown dead
and yet I wanted those names to exist,
wanted an anonymous language
– my own –
to speak of the nameless many.
What we call peace
is merely the short relief of a truce.
If a name is a way of reaching oneself,
none of these dead have reached their resting place.

There are only places, island places
from which to view the Continent
– the east – the dust
its wars raise to obfuscate
the verdict: we are not saved,
we do not save
unless with oblique courage,
with a gesture
of minimal light.

III

Per trovare la ragione di un verbo
perché ancora davvero non è tempo
e non sappiamo se accorrere o fuggire.

Fai sera come fosse dicembre
sulle casse innalzate sul cuneo del trasloco
dai forma al buio
mentre il cibo s'infiamma alla parete.

Queste sono le notti di pace occidentale
nei loro raggi vola l'angustia delle biografie
gli acini scuri dei ritratti, i cartigli dei nomi.

Ci difende di lato un'altra quiete
come un peso marino nella iuta
piegato a lungo, con disperazione.

III

To discover the reason for a verb
because truly it isn't yet time
and we don't know whether to rush towards it or take flight.

Make evening come as though in December
over the tea-chests on the brink of removal.
Give form to darkness
while the food flames up against the wall.

These are the nights of Western peace
and flying in their rays are the narrowness of lives,
the dark berries of portraits, the scrolls of names.

A different quietness shields us on one side
like a marine weight wrapped in jute
and folded carefully, with desperation.

IV

Correva verso un rifugio, si proteggeva la testa.
Apparteneva a un'immagine stanca
non diversa da una donna qualsiasi
che la pioggia sorprende.

Non volevo dire della guerra
ma della tregua
meditare sullo spazio e dunque sui dettagli
la mano che saggia il muro, la candela per un attimo accesa
e – fuori – le fulgide foglie.
Ancora un recinto con spine confuse ad altre spine
spine di terra che bruciano i talloni.

Ciò che si stende il peso del prima
e il precipitare del poi:
questo io chiamo tregua
misura che rende misura lo spavento
metro che non protegge.

Vicino a tregua è transito
da un luogo andare a un altro luogo
senza una vera meta
senza che nulla di quel moto possa chiamarsi viaggio
distrazione di volti
mentre batte la pioggia.

Alla tregua come al treno occorre la pianura
un sogno di orizzonte
con alberi levati verso il cielo
uniche lance, sentinelle sole.

IV

She was running towards shelter, covering her head.
She belonged in that commonplace image,
indistinguishable from any other
woman surprised by rain.

I didn't wish to speak of the war
but of the truce,
to meditate on that space and so on detail:
the hand that tests a wall, the candle lit just for a moment
and – outside – the shining leaves.
It remains a fenced enclosure with a tangle of barbs,
thorns of earth that burn the talons.

That which stretches between the weight of before
and the fell sweep of then:
is what I call truce,
a measure that measures but gives
no protection from fear.

Close to truce is transit –
going from one place to another
without any specific aim
so nothing in that movement could call itself a journey,
a distraction of faces
while the rain beats down.

For the truce as for the train what's required
is a flatland, a dream of the horizon
with trees lifted into the sky,
solitary lances, lonely sentinels.

VI

Non esiste innocenza in questa lingua
ascolta come si spezzano i discorsi
come anche qui sia guerra
diversa guerra
ma guerra – in un tempo assetato.

Per questo scrivo con riluttanza
con pochi sterpi di frase
stretti a una lingua usuale
quella di cui dispongo per chiamare
laggiù perfino il buio
che scuote le campane.

C'è una finestra nella notte
con due sagome scure addormentate
brune come gli uccelli
il cui corpo indietreggia contro il cielo.

Scrivo con pazienza
all'eternità non credo
la lentezza mi viene dal silenzio
e da una libertà – invisibile –
che il Continente non conosce
l'isola di un pensiero che mi spinge
a restringere il tempo
a dargli spazio
inventando per quella lingua il suo deserto.

La parola si spacca come legno
come un legno crepita di lato
per metà fuoco
per metà abbandono.

VI

This language has no innocence
– listen to how speeches break up
as if also here there were a war
a different war but war
all the same – in a time of drought.

And so I write with reluctance
with a few dry stumps of phrases
boxed into humdrum language
which I arrange so as to call out
down there as far as the dark
that sounds the bells

There's a window in the night
with two dark shapes asleep
dun as birds
whose bodies draw back against the sky.

I write with patience
to the eternity I don't believe in.
Slowness comes to me from silence
and from a freedom – invisible –
which the Continent is unaware of
– the island of a thought which spurs me
to shorten time
to give it space
inventing the desert for that language.

The word splits like wood
like a piece of wood cracked on one side,
part the effect of fire
part of neglect.

VIII

Forse se moriamo è per questo?
Perché l'aria liquida dei giorni
scuota di colpo il tempo e gli dia spazio
perché l'invisibile, il fuoco delle attese
si spalanchi nell'aria
e bruci quello che ci sembrava
il nostro solo raccolto?

VIII

If we die perhaps it's for this?
So the liquid air of days
may suddenly shake time and give it space,
so what's invisible, the fire of waiting,
may fling itself wide open in the air
and burn what seemed to us
our only harvest.

XIII

(a Nathan Zach)

Anche questi sono versi di guerra
composti mentre infuria, non lontano, non vicino
seduti di sghembo a un tavolo rischiarato da lumi
mentre cingono le porte di palme
anche questo è un canto verso Dio
che chini lo sguardo su noi vermi e ci travolga
amati e non amati.
Non una tregua – un dono per questa terra folgorata.

XIII

(to Nathan Zach)

These too are war poems
composed while it rages, not far off, not nearby,
seated askew at a table lit by lamps
whilst the doors are hung with palm fronds.
This too is a song lifted towards God
to let his gaze descend on his worms and overwhelms us,
loved and unloved alike.
Not a truce – a gift
for this thunderstruck earth.

a mia figlia
(19-11-1993)

Davvero come adesso, l'ulivo sul balcone
il vento che trasmuta le nubi. Oltre il secolo
nelle sere a venire quando né tu né io ci saremo
quando gli anni saranno rami
per spingere qualcosa senza meta
nelle sere in cui altri
si guarderanno come oggi
nel sonno – nel buio
come calchi di vulcano curvi nella cenere bianca.

Piego il lenzuolo, spengo l'ultima luce.
Lascio che le tue tempie battano piano le coperte
che si genufletta la notte
sul tuo veloce novembre.

to my daughter
(19/11/1993)

Just as it is now, the olive tree on the balcony,
the wind which reshapes the clouds. In the next
century, in the evenings to come when neither
you nor I will be here, when the years will be branches
aimlessly pushing some thing forward,
in the evenings when others
will watch one another as today,
sleepily – in the dark
like curled figures wrapped in the volcano's white ash.

I fold down the sheet, switch off the last light,
and let your temples quietly beat under the covers,
so the night will kneel
beside your headlong November.

*   *   *

Se ho scritto è per pensiero
perché ero in pensiero per la vita
per gli esseri felici
stretti nell'ombra della sera
per la sera che di colpo crollava sulle nuche.
Scrivevo per la pietà del buio
per ogni creatura che indietreggia
con la schiena premuta a una ringhiera
per l'attesa marina – senza grido – infinita.

Scrivi, dico a me stessa
e scrivo io per avanzare più sola nell'enigma
perché gli occhi mi allarmano
e mio è il silenzio dei passi, mia la luce deserta
– da brughiera –
sulla terra del viale.

Scrivi perché nulla è difeso e la parola *bosco*
trema più fragile del bosco, senza rami né uccelli
perché solo il coraggio può scavare
in alto la pazienza
fino a togliere peso
al peso nero del prato.

*　*　*

If I've written it's for thought
because my thoughts are troubled about life
it's for those happy beings
close in the evening shadow
for the evening which at a stroke
collapsed on the napes of necks
for every creature that backs away
pressing its spine against the railings
and for the waiting on the tide – without a cry – endless.

Write, I say to myself
and I write to press onwards more solitary into the enigma
because eyes disturb me
and the silence of footsteps is my own, and mine the desert light
– light of the moorlands –
on the earth of the avenue.

Write because nothing is protected and the word *wood*
shakes more frailly than the wood itself, without branches or birds
because only courage can excavate
patience in the heights
until it takes the weight away
from the meadow's black weight.

*   *   *

Volevo che il mio amore non finisse
che resistesse intero – in disaccordo
perfino col ricordo e ignorasse il corpo
che da me si scostava
che ne ignorasse distanza e indifferenza
e fosse cosa mia doppiamente intrecciata
cesta di giunco e aria, cesta per acqua
forma che la mano conosce
e che la storia medita quando – così di rado
per questo raramente sacra – salva un bambino dal suo Nilo.
Così a volte fanno canestri i pazzi
per il silenzio – credo – che sale dagli spazi
per quella paglia
che le dita oscurano
per quel nodo terreno
di aria e di materia.

*   *   *

I wanted my love not to end,
but to resist intact – at odds, even,
with memory – to disregard the fact his body
had withdrawn itself from me,
disregard the distance and indifference,
and to be my own, a doubly woven
basket of bulrushes and air, basket for water
– a shape the hand knows, which history seldom
takes account of, except for when – rare enough
to be be thought holy – it saves an infant from his Nile.
So sometimes the mad make wicker baskets
for the silence, I think, which rises out of space,
for that straw
which fingers darken,
for that earthly knot
of air and matter.

* * *

nella morte di Amelia Rosselli

Se non fosse che questo: giungere a un luogo
esattamente pronunciarne il nome, essere a casa.

Felice inverno adesso che il nuovo inverno è passato
da un inizio per noi ancora senza nome
non diverso dal varco estivo di reti
forse, un cerchio debole di lumi.
Intorno, solo piante
che non avresti fatto in tempo a scansare
acqua soffiata sulle pietre – grandine
che mai sapremo se è arrivata col suono
che faceva sui tetti là nel tuo tempo
nella bianca, umana pulizia dei bagni.
Finora solo passi recisi
che forse ascolti con ardente silenzio
e aria tra gli aranci mossi piano dai vivi.

Vedi qui nulla per la prima volta si perde.
Stamattina hanno battuto la terra
fredda – colma della gioia dell'acqua
ha dimenticato per te
la sbarra della sedia, la nuca rovesciata
il vento del cortile.
Così felice notte ora che di nuovo è notte
e non è vero che il gelo resti
e abbassi piano il pensiero
forse uno scatto invece schiude qualcosa in alto
molto in alto
una nota

* * *

at the death of Amelia Rosselli

If it were only this: to reach a place,
to say its name unfalteringly, to be at home.

Happy winter now a new winter has passed
from a beginning still nameless to us,
no different perhaps than a gap opening between
summer's fishing nets, a circle of faint lights.
In your present neighbourhood, only plants
you wouldn't have had time to push aside,
water breeze-blown onto the tombstones – hail
we'll never know if it fell with the sound
it had on the roof tiles there in your time,
in the bright white human cleanliness of bathrooms.
Till now only the clipped sound of footsteps overhead
which perhaps you hear in ardent silence,
the air between the orange trees the living gently displace.

Now – a first for you – see how nothing is lost.
This morning they flattened with a spade the cold
earth – brimming with the joy of water –
that has forgotten on your behalf
the back of the chair, your twisted neck,
wind in the courtyard.
So happy night now there's a new night
and it isn't true that the ice remains
and slowly lessens the pulse of thought.

Or else, perhaps, a sudden snap discloses something
high up above –
a note

oltre il becco oltre gli occhi lucenti di un uccello
una scheggia di collina – quella laggiù
serrata al tetto verde-bronzo della chiesa.
Felice notte a te
per sempre priva di abisso, una steppa dell'anima-sommessa
dove l'ulivo si piega senza suono
Gerusalemme della quiete
della quiete e del tronco che cerchia e incide la morte
che la succhia nel vuoto e nel vuoto la getta
e la macera piano.

Non ho voce, né canto
ma una lingua intrecciata di paglia
una lingua di corda e sale chiuso nel pugno
e fitto in ogni fessura
nel cancello di casa che batte sul tumulo duro dell'alba
dal buio al buio
per chi resta
per chi ruota.

far beyond a bird's beak, far higher than its shining eyes:
a frayed edge of hillside – that one down there
locked to the church's bronze-green roof.
Happy night to you
forever bereft of the abyss, in a flatland of the subdued spirit
where the olive tree soundlessly bends,
Jerusalem of quiet,
of quiet and of the trunk death circles and engraves
which sucks it into the void and in the void casts it out
and slowly chews it.

I have no voice, no song at all,
only a language mixed with straw,
a language of rope and salt clenched in the fist
and to fill every crack
in the house gate that bangs on the hard tumulus of dawn
from darkness to darkness
for whoever remains, for whoever
keeps turning.

Il catalogo della gioia
Catalogue of Joy

2003

Aprile, La Maddalena. Resti di sogni

Chiaro, ma denso come immaginiamo sia
il tempo di un'aurora boreale
una scena di pesca silenziosa.
L'acqua nel ghiaccio. L'amo che scende con cautela.

(Soffio sulle Bocche, volo in avanti sugli scogli
su fino al freddo, ai continenti, alla tua casa, al cuore
di legno dell'armadio, all'ormai sconosciuto, cupo letto.
Il tuo viso è l'arco di noce della porta
il mio l'alba che invade la finestra).

Una figura oscilla dentro il sonno.
E' l'ubriaco che ieri nel vento della banchina
si dondolava cantando a bocca chiusa.

April, La Maddalena Island. Dream Fragments

Clear, but thickly strewn as we imagine
the Aurora Borealis,
a soundless fishing scene.
Water in ice. A bait gingerly lowered.

(I blow on the Bocche, fly ahead over the rocks
on through the cold, across continents, to your house,
to the wardrobe's wooden heart, to that now
unknown and darkened bed.
Your face is the door's walnut arch,
mine the dawn encroaching on the window.)

A figure wavers in the dream.
It's the drunkard who yesterday on the windy dock
was rocking and singing with his mouth shut.

Maggio, La Maddalena. Resti di sogni

Contro l'arco dei monti
la curva del tuo petto
che dava pace al mio spazio.
I tuoi ordini lenti dentro il sogno, la voce che diceva:
'voltati, sdraiati qui sulla spiaggia
come se nel cammino si scavasse un letto.'
Obbedendo e trovando pace in quel rovescio
mentre la mia schiena si piega, il corpo pesa
e tu stendi gigli selvaggi sulla sabbia.

May, La Maddalena Island. Dream Fragments

Against the arch of the mountains
the curve of your chest
which brought calm to my space.
Your slow commands within the dream, the voice
which said: 'Turn over, stretch out on this beach
as though you'd hollowed a bed from the path.'
Obeying and finding peace in that overturning
while my spine bends, my body weighs
and you arrange wild lilies on the sand.

Settembre 2001. Arcipelago della Maddalena, isola di S. Stefano

questa piccola isola forata sott'acqua dai sommergibili americani,
dove mio bisnonno piantò viti e agrumi
costruì stalle e portò dieci vacche dal Continente.
I loro zoccoli tremanti sulla barca, il vento sui dorsi
colpiti fino allora solo dalle piogge del nord.
Sono ancora lì, le corna miste a sabbia
gli scheletri profondi, stretti agli scogli senza più paura,
senza più distinzione tra i pascoli e il mare.

September 2001. Maddalena Archipelago. Island of S. Stefano

This small island riven underwater by U.S. submarines,
where my great-grandfather planted citrus fruits and vines,
built cowsheds and brought ten cows from the mainland.
Their trembling hoofs on the boat, the wind on their backs
only struck till then by rain from the north.
They're still there, horns mingled with the sand,
deep-rooted skeletons, close up to the rocks, no longer afraid,
no longer distinguishing pasture from sea.

Una terra

Tonda, gelida con i suoi oceani, trasparente
come una cellula sotto il microscopio
eppure orizzontale con monti posati saldamente sopra i prati
con la lingua dei fiumi e il mare steso.

Solo a volte sospetto la vertigine:
ruotiamo più veloci. Dormendo grido 'cado'
e là sento lo spazio, il nero, le stelle sulla nuca
lo spavento che vomita se stesso in mille sfere.

'Oh quello è l'inferno', dici e ti addormenti.
Medito sull'inferno allora. Basta che muova il peso della tenda
facendo scorrere gli anelli lungo il vetro. Vedo con esattezza:
un filo di formiche la loro marcia, la grande notte stellata.

Provo a prendere l'inferno per un lembo
(un po' di nero, il vuoto, lo spavento)
per farlo vorticare nel cortile
perché l'abete ruoti fino al cielo,
per essere l'insetto che sono sempre stata:
che nasce e si dimentica nell'aria.

Earth

Round, frozen with its oceans, transparent
like a cell under the microscope
and yet horizontal with mountains planted firmly above fields
with the tongues of rivers and the leagues of sea.

Every now and then I have an inkling of vertigo:
we're turning faster. Asleep, I cry out 'I'm falling'
and then feel space, blackness, the stars at the nape of my neck,
fear which spews itself out in a thousand spheres.

'Oh that would be hell' you say, and doze off.
So I meditate on hell. It's enough if the curtain's weight
Tugs the rings along the glass...with precision I see
the marching of a line of ants, the vast starry night.

I try to take hold of hell by its border
(a strip of black, emptiness, fear)
to make it whirl in the courtyard
so the fir tree wheels up into the sky,
to make me the insect that I've always been:
that's born and forgets itself in the air.

f

È la lettera della felicità terrena del soffio che fugge dalle labbra, è la fiducia dei fiori che si flettono quando scende il sole, ma è anche la lettera del fulmine, della fiamma che fende il buio.

'Fa freddo,' diciamo e la f si raddoppia nello stesso fiato della bocca sul fuoco.

i

È la lettera dell'ilarità, del riso infantile ma anche del raglio degli asini che sembrano ridere e poi piangono o misteriosamente invocano. Le labbra si tendono, la lingua resta immobile.

La testa si inclina indietro in un inno incompiuto.

f

Is the letter of felicity, of earthly joys, of the breath's flight from the lips, its fading; it's the faith of flowers that fold when the sun sets, but it's also the letter of the lightning flash, of the flame that, flickering, cleaves the dark.

'It's freezing' we say, and the f doubles in the same breath that feeds the fire.

i

Is the letter of hilarity, of the infantile laugh but also of the donkeys braying when they seem to laugh and then weep or mysteriously invoke. The lips extend. The tongue remains immobile.

The head imperceptibly tilts back in an incomplete hymn.

Arcipelago (un collasso)

Rosso e grigio, una corona spezzata di granito e sale
un soffio nel cuore di ogni scoglio.

Sono caduta sotto poche nuvole
un giorno di piena primavera
con un cespuglio piegato sotto il corpo
e l'intero promontorio sulla nuca.
Avevo la sabbia nelle orecchie, la zampa
del cane incerta sulle tempie.
Uno smottamento simile a quello che conosciamo in sogno
l'istante in cui il moto sembra trovare l'enigma dello spazio.

Tutte le isole volavano
riproducendo con esattezza il vuoto tra le pietre
riempiendosi di vento a ogni sosta
i sassi scattavano fischiando
come fionde fino al gelo dei piedi
e il fiato era un tronco con foglie da inghiottire
a occhi stretti, fino alle radici.

Prima ci fu la casa, grigia, perfetta dentro il sole
assi sconnesse, vecchi chiodi, una sedia,
poi quel fischio misto a voci
due bambini e la lingua del cane
come un tocco d'infinito sulla gola.

Forse fu questo che mostrò al destino
come ancora mi ardesse la linea della vita

quando la mano scorticata si mosse
a scacciare una mosca
che puntò decisa verso il cielo.

Archipelago (heart failure)

Red and grey; a broken crown of salt and granite.
A breeze seeping from the heart of the rocks.

I fell under the few clouds
one day in the full springtime
with a bush bent under my body
and the whole promontory at my neck.
I had sand in my ears, the dog's paw
uneasy at my temples.
A disturbance we know from dreams
when movement meets the enigma of space.

All the islands flew apart
recreating exactly the void between the stones,
refueling themselves with wind at every stop.
The boulders sprang off whistling
like slings as far as my frozen feet
and breathing was a bristling trunk to swallow
with eyes tight shut
as far as the roots.

Before there was the house, grey and perfect in the sunlight,
but out of kilter – old nails, a chair –
then that whistling interspersed with voices,
two children and a dog's tongue
like a touch of the infinite at my throat.

It was this perhaps that showed fate
how the lifeline still burned in me,
when the skinned hand moved
to brush away a fly which then
betook itself unflinchingly skywards.

Coraggio

La cucina è un promontorio. Le pentole sono scogli divorati da un vento-lupo che soffia e corre in cerchio nell'isola. La ringhiera della finestra è una raffica grigia, sua compagna nostra sorella aguzza. Appena svegli noi siamo gli uccelli chini sul lavabo, stanchi della migrazione notturna, confusi dai razzi che percuotono i sogni.

In tutto il quadro è inverno.
Nella musica della radio rintocca la grandine.
Il suo bianco vibra sulle antenne e il balcone.
Con il suo muso di nuvola pietosa
l'alba ci spinge alla vita.

Courage

The kitchen is a promontory. The pans are rocks devoured by a
wolf wind that scours the island for prey. The window's railing is
a grey gust of rain – his companion, our angular sister. Just
woken, we are birds leaning over the sink tired from night
migrations, dazzled by flares that drum on our dreams.

Winter fills the whole picture.
With the radio music we hear the clatter of hail.
Its whiteness quivers on the aerials and the balcony.
With its compassionate muzzle of cloud
dawn nudges us into life.

*   *   *

Silenzio notturno. Quando ci si alza nel buio estivo
e gli alberi restano senza vento oltre la porta spalancata.
Quando le stanze respirano piano e il mare si unisce ai gerani.
Rosso e cobalto e ancora rosso
nei fari del porto
nei traghetti che sfavillano e aspettano.

Silenzio mattutino. Una qualità dei passi sul selciato
delle voci. E' il suono delle saracinesche
che si sollevano sui negozi intatti: un segnale di pace
l'annuncio dello shofar nel giorno.

Sole silenzioso sulle coperte, sui pavimenti
sulle tazze della colazione e lo smalto del vassoio.
Sì. Non benedetto abbastanza ogni risveglio silenzioso e vivo
non ancora malato non ancora schiavo.

*   *   *

Night silence. When you get up in the summer dark
and trees hang in the windlessness beyond the door flung wide.
When rooms breathe slowly and the sea blends with the geraniums.
Red and cobalt, then red once more
from the harbour's hazard lights,
from the ferries that glitter and wait.

Morning silence. A resonance in footsteps on paving stones,
in voices. It's the sound of shutters being raised
on untouched shops – a sign of peace:
clear peal from the day's shofar.

Silent sun on blankets, on floors,
on breakfast cups and the tray's enamel.
Yes. Never blessed enough each new awakening
not yet ailing, not yet enslaved.

Dal balcone del corpo
From the Body's Balcony

2007

Contro Scaurum

No ischio iscrivere de Roma.
Meda belluria, dechidu, mutas 'e linu.
Forzis gòi –sunt binti seculos– pessaint cuddos sardos
bennitos a dimandare zusstissia contra Scauro.

'Zente chene ide…terra ue peri su mele est 'ele'

Gòi nàrriat Cicero in faeddu suo. Ora, in mesu petras
bortat suo lumene, lestru, minutu. Ma sicutera
morint sos distimonzos, s' ape tribulat.
Reghet su mele: limba e'lidone, gardu et sale.

Against Scaurus

How can I write of Rome in one or seven days
– a glut of beauty, taste and linen tunics.
Maybe those Sards, 20 centuries ago, felt this
when they came to plead for justice against Scaurus.

'A truthless people…land where even the honey is gall'

Cicero said in his oration. But his name, now,
tiny and rapid, flits among the stones, and just as
then, witnesses die, the bee labours on.
Honey endures – a tongue of salt, arbutus, thistle.

In 54 BC, Scaurus, proconsul in Sardinia, was accused of extortion and of being the cause of the suicide of a woman he had raped. The Sards came to Rome to testify, but Scaurus had as his defence lawyer Cicero, who poured scorn on these unkempt figures, covered with animal skins, bewildered among the columns of the refined Tribunal. Although apparently guilty, Scaurus was absolved.

Limba

Non tenes baùle 'e istrisinare in supr'e nie
Ma unu cane a trémula in s'iscuriù

Limba-matre ses triste
S'azu s'inniéddigat in sa sartàine

Sa mùghit'anziat
Sos ventos si coffundent.
Eolo survat et Babele s'isparghet.

Fiza-limba tràchitas a ghineperu
Una tremita tua naschinde
Est ch'astula de livrina in mes'a isteddos

et sas nues, sas nues a sa thurpas fughint
iscanzellande dae chelu onzi zenìas

Tongue

You own no coffin to drag across the snow,
just a dog shivering in the dark.

Mother-tongue you're heavyhearted;
garlic blackens in the copper pan.

A low drone rises from the hearth.
Winds tangle random and athwart.
Aeolus blows but Babel's left alive.

Daughter-tongue: creak of the juniper.
Your shudder at birth's a shard chipped off
a storm among the planets

and the clouds, the clouds blindly race
obliterating from the skies
all trace of lineage.

Attittos

I

Tòrrami a fizu tuo
terra bestia 'e nieddu
cara 'e proya. Mi giamat
ma tue ses corfu 'e bistrale.
Eo non podo respondere
prena de ludu e ispina

VII

Li kerìa colare un'ispùgnia 'e ferru in su pettos
lu ferrer a samben che a una gristos
po mi lu parrer che torradu vivu

Dirges

I

Give me back your son
earth draped in black
with your face of rain. He calls me
but you're the thud of an axe.
Snared in mud and thorn
I can't call back.

VII

I wanted to wash him down with an iron sponge
wound him till he bled like a christ
to fool myself he would rise again.

The two 'Dirges' are from a series of eight 'Attittos' – traditional Sardinian
verse laments improvised at the graveside by women of the family.

Tra il prima e il poi. Incidente

Il ponte si chiuse ruotando tra le luci
e subito il dono fu il dettaglio:
la forma ovale dei fiori
sul ramo dell'albero di Giuda
questo un attimo prima che il volante
ci spingesse sul tronco ai margini del bosco.

Tutto rimase intatto colmo di colore:
lillà e cobalto e un marrone sbalzato di grigio
solo incapace di soccorrere
come un ricordo usuale. Il vento
senza origine e odore. La collina
un cono nudo come il Calvario.

Sognai noi due dentro un passato prossimo, bruciante.
Poi, in modo più sfocato – in un pendio della memoria:
il viaggio, il sesso: due spettri lenti dentro i vestiti –
Mi spostai col pensiero – difficile dire come –
mentre poco distante il mondo continuava.
Di colpo il dolore prese nomi diversi
di eventi naturali come: 'uragano islandese'
o, 'fhonn di mezzanotte'.
Perfino il freddo che ci batteva i polsi
prima dello schianto sembrò degno
di una lunghissima preghiera.
Ci saremmo genuflessi– forse per sempre –
davanti al tetto di ardesia:
a quella pietra e alla finestra giallo-ocra,
un oro dei Maya nel tramonto...
Ci saremmo...

Between Then and Now: Accident

The bridge shut revolving between the lights
and suddenly the gift was in the detail:
the oval shape of the flowers
on the Judas tree's branch – all this
a moment before the wheel slung us
 against a trunk at the wood's edge.

Everything remained brimming with colour:
lilac and cobalt and a grey-etched brown,
only none of this of any use
as retrospect might be. The wind
without origin or odour. The hill
a bare cone like Calvary.

I dreamt we two were held burning in the tense of a recent past.
Then, more out-of-focus, on memory's slope:
the trip, sex: two ghosts slow moving in their clothes;
I changed position with the thought – hard to say how –
while not far off the world persisted.
Suddenly pain took on the different names
of natural events like 'Islandic hurricane'
or 'midnight Föhn'.
Even the cold that beat on our wrists
before the crash seemed worthy
of the most extended prayer.
We would be kneeling – perhaps forever –
in front of the slate roof:
before that stone and the yellow-ochre window,
the Mayan gold of sunset...

We would be...

la condizione del verbo sparì inghiottita nel clangore.
Vidi le poche nubi ferme nelle vene.

Stai andando, mi dissi, stai già leggendo all'indietro.

The conditional was swallowed by the din.
I saw a few clouds tethered stationary in our veins.

You're going away, I told myself, already you're reading backwards.

Così arrivano i delitti

Il bambino era sveglio quando hanno arrestato la madre.
Lo hanno portato via. Volevo avvertirti
ma pioveva forte, le luci erano spente.
Mi sono asciugata e rimessa a dormire. Così arrivano i delitti:
quando qualcuno sente le grida e poi torna a letto, quando non ha
        la forza.
Colpa del corpo che ama il piacere, del conforto che scaccia il dolore
e preferisce una coperta e un cuscino all'agire.
Il bambino gridava. La pioggia copriva la luna.
Dormendo piangevo di pena ma il mio corpo non si alzava.
L'acqua colpiva il tetto pesava sulle travi
e io sognando fuggivo con le orecchie fitte di lana.

In This Way Crimes Come About

The baby was awake when they came to arrest his mother.
They took him away. I wanted to warn you
but it was raining hard. The lights were all out.
I dried myself and went back to sleep. This is how
crimes come about: when someone hears a cry and then
goes back to bed, when someone hasn't the strength.
Fault of the body which loves its pleasure. Fault of comfort
that crushes pain and prefers a pillow and a duvet
to acting. The baby kept crying. Rain covered the moon.
Sleeping I wept from pain but my body stayed put.
Water struck the roof, weighed down the beams
and in my dream I fled, my ears stuffed with wool.

Coro

(a mia madre)

Non dorme, si prepara. Verranno a chiamarla la mattina.
Ha preparato una valigia, serve
per l'oscillante vita di ospedale. L'albero contro il letto
spinge le sue gemme sui rami. Lei dondola seduta.

L'uccellino dell'anima tende la gola fino a lei.
E' di legno, che importa?
dondola anche lui tra un'asta e il buio.

Chorus

(to my mother)

She stays awake, gets ready. In the morning they'll call for her.
She's prepared a suitcase that will do
for the see-saw life of the ward. Against the bed
the tree puts forth its buds. She rocks to and fro in her chair.

The bird of the soul extends his throat towards her.
He's made of wood, but what does that matter?
He too rocks between a perch and the dark.

Amore e corvo

Ho visto un corvo abbassarsi
su uno dei gradini della scala:
è stato un miracolo di nerità lucente
un lungo inchiostro sul bianco della pietra.
L'intera discesa – mia e del corvo – sapeva di betulla e miele.
I nostri corpi – del corvo e mio – erano svelti e vecchi.
– Guardandolo muoversi mi accorsi
di quanto il nero fosse offuscato
di qualche macchia e di come l'andatura fosse
incerta. Anche le mie gambe, qua e là macchiate dall'età e dal sole
erano un segno come per lui quel cieco saltellare.
Eppure entrambi in amore amavamo: lui le poche lucide piume
io un residuo di grazia:
l'affusolarsi delle gambe fino ai piedi e i piedi leggermente contratti
fragili (come i suoi) con artigli cremisi.
Ora voliamo lui verso il cielo e io verso la terra
laggiù sotto la scala che mi aspetta:
un lembo ancora senza colore, ma con muschio e pietre
un continente inesplorato.

È un bene che vacilla.

Il cielo chiude il corvo.
La pietra mi scricchiola sui passi un'orchestra di ghiaia.
Inghiotte parti di me. Rode i talloni.

Love and the Crow

I saw a crow climb down one
    step of a flight of stairs:
a revelation of shining blackness,
a long plume of ink on the white stone.
The whole descent – mine and the crow's – was redolent of birch
            trees and honey.
Our bodies – the crow's and mine – were lean and old.
Watching him move I saw
how stained his black was, how
hesitant his whole deportment.
My legs too, stained here and there by age and the sun,
were a sign, as that blind hopping was for him.
And yet both of us were enamoured: he of his few shining feathers
I of what grace remained:
the way my legs tapered to my feet and my feet were lightly tensed
and frail (like his) with crimson claws.
Then we fly off, he skywards, I towards the earth
that waits for me, down there, beneath the steps:
a patch of earth, still colourless, but with stones and moss,
an unexplored continent.

It's a wavering grace.

The sky closes over the crow.
The stone creaks under my steps, an orchestra of gravel.
It swallows parts of me. Wears down my talons.

Coro

Sì non siamo quello che ci piace credere
ma solo l'altro versante della storia:
quando non serve agire quando le cose vanno bene.
Cosa di quello che succede ad altri saremmo in grado di sopportare?
Quanta ipocrisia serve a foderarci il petto?
I fiori esplodono nelle aiuole. Il fuoco vive sugli oggetti in frantumi.
Le parole che gli esseri umani si scambiano sono solo richiami.
Un cane corre sulla sua sola zampa: risorge a ogni guerra
            dall'immondizia.
Salta sui cadaveri. Da lontano lo diresti sano
e i colori dei rottami e della plastica li diresti
dalie, vasi di basilico tra i muri.

Chorus

Yes we are not what we'd like to think we are
but the other side of history:
when it's no use doing anything, when things are going well.
How much of what happens to others could we bear?
How much hypocrisy would keep the heart fur-lined?
The flowers explode in the flowerbeds. Fire leaps alive from
        splintered things.
Words that people exchange are only warnings.
A dog runs on its single paw: it rises again from the rubbish of
        every war.
It jumps on the bodies. From a distance you'd say it was well
and you'd guess that the colours of wreckage and plastic
were dahlias, pots of basil between the walls.

All'angelo, dopo la cacciata

Mi spingi dicendo: 'Si sta bene al buio'.
Guardo i gerani sulla finestra cieca
penso: li annaffierò comunque
fino alla schiarita di una foglia
all'unghia di un colore,
ma la lingua che a un tratto mi hai tagliato
non può pensare a lungo.
'Perché' avevo chiesto all'inizio.
Adesso che non parlo e ho solo gli occhi
dici che sono fatta per le tenebre.
Leggi con la tua voce di mattone rauco
cosa è scritto sul muro, per me, per te, noi tutti:
'Spargo le vostre opere, le do in pasto agli uccelli
col miglio sul balcone. Vi basta un po' di pane
uno sgabello. Forse avete dimenticato: è una prigione.'

To the Angel, after the Expulsion

You shove me, saying 'It's not so bad in the dark'.
I look at the geraniums in the bricked-up window
and think: I'll water them anyway
till a leaf unfurls, a bright
petal the shape of a tiny nail,
but my tongue which you've abruptly cut out
can't think very far.
'Why' I'd asked at first.
Now I can't speak and have only my eyes,
you say that I'm made for the dark.
You read with your voice of raucous brick
what's written on the wall for me, for you, for us all:
'I will scatter your works and with some millet
feed them to the birds on the balcony.
A little bread and a stool to sit on
is all you'll get. Perhaps it's escaped you:
where you are is a prison.'

Coro

(a M.)

Venite pensieri vi penseremo a fondo ora che è mattino.
La luce vi fa sembrare tanto forti da raschiare il buio
come se avessimo un coccio e la notte fosse cuoio.

C' è un geco sul granito.
Il suo ventre oscilla come acqua di fonte.
È spaventato. È attento.
Aspetta senza capire.
Come succede a noi
quando un saluto di colpo si trasforma in addio.

Chorus

(to M.)

Come thoughts we'll think you through now morning's here.
In the light you look tough enough to scrape the darkness off
as if we held a crock sherd and the night was thick leather.

A gecko's clamped to the wall,
belly wavering like fountain water.
It's alert and scared.
Waiting without comprehension,
as can happen to us
when without warning a greeting turns into farewell.

Getsemani

Non una luce ultraterrena
ma un bagliore di pentole di rame
un metallo interiore
(a croce mio malgrado)
in un calvario di oggetti del mattino:
la busta di plastica, gli ombrelli
un raggio di bottiglie
più lattee nella brina.
C'è una pena che ignoro
se mi aspetta in un orto di buio, di paura
o più semplicemente nel cortile
vicino al tronco dell'albero di Giuda.

Gethsemane

Not a supernatural light
but the gleam of a copper pan
an interior metal
(in the shape of a cross I'd not want to bear)
– a Calvary of things for the morning:
the plastic bag, umbrellas,
a row of bottles left out
milkily webbed with ice.

I'm not sure if the pain to come
is waiting for me in the garden of darkness, of fear,
or more simply in the courtyard
beside the trunk of the Judas tree.

Cana

Scopri che nella cantina addetta a dormitorio c'erano giocattoli, materassi, taniche d'acqua, riserve di cibo. Da occidente guardi la distanza tra noi macerie e le nozze, tra la polvere e il rame, tra la tela che non copre i piedi dei morti e il ruscello di seta sulla schiena della sposa.

Allora scrivi per terra un'ultima volta, trasformando il sangue in vino e poi di nuovo in acqua. Chiedi che tutto si sciolga. Chiami la pioggia. Scagli il bastone.

Cana

In the canteen turned into a dormitory you find there were toys, mattresses, jerrycans of water, a stash of food. To the west, you see the distance between us – the rubble – and the wedding feast, between the dust and the copper, between the cloth that doesn't quite cover the feet of the dead and the river of silk on the bride's back.

Then you write on the ground one final time, turning the blood to wine and then back to water. You pray that everything dissolves. You call forth the rain, chuck away the stick.

Coro

(a R.)

Siamo lo schermo, il corpo, questa luce
che taglia la scrittura.
Siamo l'alfabeto che scolora.
Vattene dico alla parola
cosa dubbiosa lasciami
cancella subito me stessa
fai che un'altra ti prenda e ti raccolga
che mi sgombri dal tempo
e faccia nulla della mia persona
la privi come vuole di lamento
le scavi un vuoto aperto solo al vento.

Chorus

(to R.)

We are the screen, the body, this light
which cuts the writing.
We're the alphabet that fades.

Go I say to the word
unsteady thing be gone
cancel myself at a stroke
let some other woman select you
and let me be free of time
and make nothing of my person
deprive her as you see fit of lament
dig in her an open gap for the wind.

Anestesie

Ci sono le creature che chiedono – non importa se in malafede
(come mi dicevano da piccola, per consolarmi).
I ridotti in schiavitù, tutte le voci calpestate che ci assordano.
Non più tardi di un'ora fa,
non più lontano di un braccio di mare e poca costa.
Eppure esiste il modo di sopportare. Basta la notte (le gocce si
prendono la sera): l'anima si ispessisce, velocemente si forma la
crosta e la mattina si può uscire, attraversare la città in relativa
calma, sordità e cecità. Solo lembi di ciò che è bruto fuori di noi:
un pezzo di camicia, un colore, una mano, un grumo di fastidio,
una folata di odio.
Su tutto l'anestesia del farmaco, la percezione del dolore
trasportata all'esterno,
vista dal balcone del corpo.
Da lassù tutto è lontano. Chi grida e cosa dice. Forse non grida,
forse non parla.
Non si riesce a vedere. Spariscono i primi piani.
Io e loro siamo sagome che si muovono in un bosco.
Come distinguere un bombardamento dai fuochi di artificio?
(chiese mia nonna che era cieca, sentendo le navi esplodere
        nel porto.)
Come decifrare le immagini:
è un film o davvero quei corpi si gettano nel vuoto?

Anaesthetics

There are creatures who beg – no matter whether in bad faith,
as they'd tell me when I was a child to console me:
those reduced to slavery, all the downtrodden voices that deafen us.
No later than an hour ago, no further away
than a stretch of sea with just a foundering glimpse of the coast.

Yet there are ways of to live with this. To get through the night it's
enough to take a few medicinal drops in the evening: the soul
thickens, a scab quickly forms and by morning you can go out,
cross the city, relatively calm, deaf and blind. Only scraps of what
assails us gets through: shred of shirt, a colour, a hand, congealed
annoyance, a gust of hate.
    On all this descends the pharmacy of anaesthesia; the perception
    of pain is exported to the outer realm
    and seen from the body's balcony.

From up there, everything's far off. Who cries and what
they say. Perhaps they don't cry, don't speak.
One can't quite see. The foreground disappears.
All of us are shapes moving in a wood.

How can you tell a bombardment from a firework display?
my grandmother, who was blind, asked, hearing the ships blown up
      in the port.
How do we decipher the images:
is this a film or did those bodies truly launch themselves into the void?

La vita dei dettagli
The Life of Details
2009

*   *   *

Sono i piedi di un morto. A volte nelle camere ardenti li legano
con un filo di nylon perché non si divarichino. Qui sono allineati
su un marmo rosso venato di marmo bianco: la pietra dell'unzione
su cui lo avrebbero messo prima di ungere il corpo. In origine il
marmo era solo rosso, le lacrime – dice un vangelo apocrifo – lo
hanno solcato di bianco.

Il pittore tenne con sé il quadro fino alla fine insieme alla sua
collezione di monete antiche. Quando lo dipinse aveva appena perso
due figli: Federico e Girolamo.

Vedo la sua vita intirizzire, secca come una ciotola di tempere.
Rivedo me stessa davanti a piedi simili.

Questo non è solo un Cristo morto ma il ritratto della nostra
vertigine davanti a ogni morte, la sua veduta aerea. L'occhio percorre
un paese deserto.

Devo smettere le forze mi abbandonano.

Mantegna, *Cristo morto* (1480-1490 *ca.*)

* * *

They are a dead man's feet. Sometimes in funeral parlours they tie them with a thread of nylon so the legs don't spread. Here they are aligned on a red marble slab that's veined with white: the mortuary stone on which they would have laid him before applying unction to his body. Originally marble was only red, before tears, said an apocryphal evangelist, had furrowed it with white.

To the very end the painter kept the picture with him along with his collection of antique coins. When he painted it he had just lost two sons: Federico and Girolamo.

I see his life benumbed, dry as a bowl of tempera. I see myself in front of similar feet.

This is not only a dead Christ but a portrait of our vertigo in front of every death, its aerial view. The eye traverses an abandoned village.

I have to stop, I've no strength left in me.

Mantegna, *Dead Christ* (*c.* 1480-90)

*   *   *

Dimmi a chi appartiene questa casa in fiamme, chi lancia la sua
picca sul vuoto, quale peccato viene punito. I diavoli si accovacciano
sulle balaustre, agitano stendardi neri.

Non lontano hanno impiccato un orso, per gioco. Ronde di
sciocchi con coltelli che trafiggono le orecchie tirano insensatamente
delle carriole. Le uova si schiudono al calore infernale, poco distante
un santo si rovescia e nuota sul dorso tra onde di nuvole accese.

Hieronymus Bosch, *La torre di Babele* (1563)

*   *   *

Tell me whose house this is on fire, who's throwing his pike into the void, which sin is being punished. The devils crouch on the banisters, waving black flags.

Not far off, they've hanged a bear, for fun. Patrols of idiots with knifes stuck through their ears pointlessly drag wheelbarrows. Eggs hatch in the hellish heat; a little way off, a saint turns over and swims backstroke through waves of firelit clouds.

Hieronymus Bosch, *The Tower of Babel* (1563)

*   *   *

Hendrickje Stoffels solleva la camicia, sente l'acqua fredda sui polpacci. Le sue gambe varcheranno il ruscello. Le sue ginocchia ingrossate avanzano con uno scatto nei muscoli. Aprono un campo di colore blu a partire dal bianco-celeste della pelle. In quale pozzanghera il pittore l'avrà fatta bagnare? Il quadro è datato pochi mesi dopo la nascita della loro figlia. Hendrickje è la sua amante, la sua domestica, la sua modella. Diventa Betsabea che legge la lettera di re David completamente nuda tranne una collana. Quando muore, lui dipinge autoritratti. Rivoli e rivoli di luce a ruscello sul suo viso da ubriaco con una corona di stagnola in testa e una spada di cartone in mano.

Rembrandt, *Giovane che si bagna in un ruscello* (1655)

*　*　*

Hendrickje Stoffels lifts her chemise, feels the water cold round her calves. Her legs wade into the stream. Her chubby knees advance with a muscular jerk. A field of blue opens out from the skin's white and azure. In what puddles did the painter make her bathe? The picture is dated a few months after the birth of their daughter. Hendrickje is his lover, his maid, his model. She becomes Bathsheba reading King David's letter, utterly naked except for a necklace. When she dies, he paints self-portraits. Rivulets of light stream down his drunkard's face, a crown of tinfoil on his head, a paste-board sword in his hand.

Rembrandt, *Young Woman Bathing in a Stream* (1655)

*   *   *

Di chi sono questi occhi, di chi queste teste mozzate?
Un terrore dettagliato. Infila lo sguardo nell'immagine come infileresti la mano in una pelliccia scucita.

Brulica ma è una bocca spalancata.
Sembra tremare ma non può, è morta.

Anticipa un sacco di Burri e il panno con cui un infermiere dell'ambulanza ieri ha tamponato il sangue di un uomo in un incidente.

Théodore Géricault, *Teste mozzate* (1818)

*　　*　　*

Whose are these eyes, whose these severed heads?

A detailed terror. Slip the gaze into the image as you'd insert a hand into a ragged fur coat.

It teems but is a wide open mouth.
It seems to tremble but can't, because he's dead.

It predates one of Alberto Burri's burlap sacks and the cloth with which a nurse in the ambulance yesterday had staunched the blood of a man involved in an accident.

Théodore Géricault, *Severed Heads* (1818)

*　*　*

Pensa la fame, pensa la sete e intorno solo acqua salata. I suoi soggetti furono cavalli, pazzi e un naufragio. Preferiva l'alba alla notte.

Di chi sono questi occhi? Di una vecchia demente. Dove appare? Nella luce calva di ombre di un Museo di Lione. Il pittore le sparge la fronte di macchie grigie come ciottoli.

Cosa l'ha resa pazza?

La didascalia dice: l'invidia.

Théodore Géricault, *Alienata con monomania dell'invidia* (1822-23)

*   *   *

He thought of hunger, thought of thirst with only salt water around. His subjects were horses, the mad and a shipwreck. He preferred dawn to night.

Whose eyes are these? An old, mad woman's. Where can they be seen? In the bald, shadowless light of a museum in Lyon. The painter speckles her forehead with grey spots like pebbles.

What made her mad?

The caption says: Envy.

Théodore Géricault, Mad Woman with a Mania of Envy (1822-23)

* * *

Figlio di un barbiere, nipote di un macellaio, beniamino del pubblico, artista rispettato. Le sue nuvole sono schiuma, i suoi cieli specchi confusi dal vapore, il suo mare monta le onde con il sangue che goccia. La sua neve strappa i cespugli. Dipinse bufere, valanghe, vento, incendi, vele nere come quella di Tristano. Acqua e cieli senza conforto, nonostante la fama e la ricchezza, sotto il ricordo della madre morta pazza.

Guarda questo naufragio con le parole che nel 1875 avrebbe scritto Hopkins: «...Spazza dentro le nevi oltre il porto/ il mare scaglie-di silice, dorso-nero...».

William Turner, *Tempesta di neve, battello a vapore al largo della bocca di un porto* (1842)

*   *   *

Barber's son, butcher's nephew, national treasure, respected artist. His clouds are foam, his skies confused mirrors of mist, his sea climbs the waves with blood that drips. His snow uproots bushes. He painted storms, avalanches, wind, fires, black sails like those of Tristan. Water and skies without comfort, despite his fame and riches, toiling under the memory of his mother who died mad.

Look at this shipwreck with the words Hopkins would write in 1875:

> Into the snows she sweeps,
> Hurling the haven behind...

And the sea flint-flake, black-backed...

William Turner, *Snow Storm: Steam-Boat off a Harbour's Mouth* (1842)

* * *

Cespugli cespugli cespugli. Quanti ne incontrerai tra questi quadri. Cespugli che si chinano sull'acqua, cespugli neri di fuoco, cespugli stecchiti dalla neve.

Guarda questi rami fotografati alla Walker Gallery di Liverpool. Sembra solo un paesaggio svizzero ma il pittore meditava sulla colpa femminile, sempre la stessa: sessuale. Il quadro fa parte di un ciclo ispirato al poema 'Nirvana' di Luigi Illica. Per Illica «mala madre» sono tutte le donne che rifiutano di esserlo e peccano per desiderio. Quando fu comprato a fine Ottocento il titolo fu cambiato da 'The Punishment of Lust' in 'The Punishment of Luxury'. Adesso è semplicemente Lust. Due donne che non vedi fluttuano sulla schiena, punite dal vento. Non hanno gambe: al loro posto un unico cirro grigio nel bianco della neve, su uno sfondo di forra.

Giovanni Segantini, *Lust* (1891)

*　　*　　*

Bushes bushes bushes. How many you find in these paintings. Bushes bent over water, black bushes of fire, bushes laden with snow.

Look at these branches photographed in the Liverpool Walker Art Gallery. It seems merely a Swiss landscape but the painter was meditating on female guilt – always the same guilt: the sexual. The painting is part of a cycle inspired by Luigi Illica's poem 'Nirvana'. For Illica, the 'bad mother' is all women who refuse that role and sin through desire. When the picture was bought at the end of the nineteenth century, the title was changed from 'The Punishment of Lust' to 'The Punishment of Luxury'. Now it's simply called 'Lust'. Two woman you can't see in the detail float on their backs, punished by the wind. They have no legs: in their place is a single grey cirrus cloud set against the white of the snow, the background a ravine.

Giovanni Segantini, *Lust* (1891)

* * *

Vivendo di sogni, percorrendo le strade di New York, raccogliendo ciò che si scarta. Incollando e inchiodando. In ogni scatola l'improbabile si avvera. La nuova immagine nasce da frammenti. Un pappagallo si dondola in una scatola di legno, un teatrino di cartone ha il fondale di un bosco incantato: sulle guglie dei palazzi frusciano ramoscelli bianchi. La storia è la sagoma di un ragazzo fiorentino trasportata in una sala giochi, la geografia è l'Egitto di una ballerina. Ognuno si scava una stanza in cui potersi voltare verso un muro. Vorrei non essere stato tanto riservato – disse, poche ore prima di morire nel 1972.

La foto appiattisce il dettaglio di uno di questi oggetti. Vive nell'enigma. Non ha titolo. «È inconoscibile – scrive Charles Simic di questo artista – come le poesie di Emily Dickinson».

Joseph Cornell, *Sfondo per una fiaba* (1942)

*   *   *

Living off dreams, wandering the streets of New York, gathering what has been thrown away. Gluing and nailing. In every box the improbable comes true. The new image is born out of fragments. A parrot swings in a wooden box, a cardboard theatre has the backdrop of an enchanted forest: fine white branches rustle on the peaked roofs of palaces. History takes the form of a Florentine boy transported into a room full of games, geography is a ballerina's Egypt. Everyone excavates a room in which to turn to the wall. 'I wish I had not been so reserved,' he said, a few hours before dying in 1972.

The photo flattens the detail of one of these boxes. It has no title. It lives in the enigma. 'He's unknowable,' writes Charles Simic of this artist, 'like Emily Dickinson's poetry.'

Joseph Cornell, *Setting for a Fairy Tale* (1942)

Salva con nome
Save As
2012

Cucina

Se l'avesse vista
se avesse visto la sua forma mortale
spalancare stanotte il frigorifero
e quasi entrare con il corpo
in quella navata di chiarore,
muta bevendo latte
come le anime il sangue
spettrale soprattutto a se stessa
assetata di bianco, abbacinata
dall'acciaio e dal ferro
bruciandosi le dita con il ghiaccio

avrebbe detto non è lei. Non è
quella che morendo ho lasciato
perché mi continuasse.

Kitchen

If he had seen her
seen her mortal form tonight
open the fridge door wide
almost bundle her body into it
into that nave of brightness
dumbly drinking milk
as spirits drink blood
ghostlike even to herself
athirst for white and dazzled by
the glare of steel and iron
her fingers burnt by ice

he would have said it wasn't her. Not
the one whom dying I left
so she could live on in my place.

Casa-madre

...*a large bad picture*...

ELIZABETH BISHOP

Ricordando una cascata vista in Corsica
mia madre dipinse un grande quadro.

('A memoria...' come Baudelaire con i *Saloni*
– È vissuta a Parigi.)

È appeso sul contatore della luce
se lo scosto si inclina

manda un bagliore di acqua mista a sale.
Tutto quel bianco ha un suono

un preciso nitore (sciabolate di azzurro, verde chiaro)
che dal cielo precipita

ma le rocce scheggiate troppo in fretta
troppo aguzze e nere

stridono nella notte come mille
lavagne sotto un'unghia.

Se la luce salta
si spegne la cascata.

Il cuore allora è un lago
agitato da un palo.

Le ore che separano dall'alba
corrono schiumando dentro il buio.

La casa ci sorveglia
baltica, bianca, indifferente.

Mother House

Recalling a waterfall seen in Corsica
my mother painted a large picture.

'From memory...' as Baudelaire wrote the *Salons*
– She'd lived in Paris.

It's hung over the light-meter
– if I move it it tilts

sending out a flash of water whitened with salt.
All that white has a sound,

a precise clarity (slashed with blue, bright green)
which falls from the sky

but the rocks are strewn with too much haste,
too black and jagged,

screech in the night like a host
of scratched blackboards.

If the light fails
the waterfall will be switched off.

Then the heart is a lake
disturbed by an oar.

The hours that remain before dawn
rush foaming behind the dark.

The house surveys us
Baltic, white, indifferent.

131

Spazio dell'invecchiare

Solo la nudità alla fine ci raggiunge
esatta come la luna crescente nei capelli.
Esiste una gioia nella reticenza
e un riparo perfino in questo spazio
che ha un inizio e una fine.
Non voglio scrivere un'elegia della vecchiaia
solo dire che spingere le braccia dentro il freddo
è una prova che ha il senso di trovare il verbo in una frase.

Senti come guadagni la via del corridoio.
Non è scontato il passo col respiro.
Conta i mattoni pensando ai ciottoli di fiume
all'acqua che ti fasciava il piede
ricorda quanta tenacia c'è voluta a decifrare
le mappe dentro alle parole.

Space to Grow Old in

In the end only nudity reaches us
as a crescent moon exerts a force in hair.
There's a joy in reticence
even a shelter in this space
which has a beginning and an end.
I don't wish to write an elegy for old age
only to say that to thrust an arm into the cold
is a test that brings the relief of finding the verb in a phrase.

Feel how you've made your way along the corridor
– breath barely sufficient for the steps you take.
Count the bricks thinking of the stones in the river,
of the water that swathes your foot.
Remember how much stamina was required
to decode the maps within the words.

Malas mutas

Anti isparau in sa cara a sos duos fratros
sos gathiles incrunant sa matta
la faghen niedda prus ki s'achina in sa cupa.

Sa luna chilliat in su core de l'Isula
su silenzio irfossa in sa Bidda des gurules mortas.
Comenti in tempos de Roma
ispingherent in sos puthus sos mortorzus
catrassandendi pustis de' vinditta.

Como cusint su piumu
ke fat drittu s'oru
de sa beste de prantu.

Bad Tidings

They shot the two brothers in the face.
The napes of their necks bend the bush down,
and make it darker than grapes in a barrel.

The moon rocks inside the island's heart.
Silence digs a ditch in Dead Throat Gulch.
As in Roman times, they dump carrion into pits
that smoulder with vendettas year after year.

Now lead is sewn into the hemlines
to make the widows' weeds
hang sheer and straight.

8-8.

povera morte sei...'

AMELIA ROSSELLI

Davvero povera cosa sei morte
se hai lasciato che tanto mi avvicinassi a lui
(se dunque a te) mentre moriva
se mi hai spaventato così poco
da darmi un'oncia di sonno vicino al suo cuscino.
Creatura piccola sei se dall'infanzia a oggi hai fatto
di te stessa una siepe scolpita da cesoie:
(ora un muso di gallo, ora di cane)
che basta poco a scavalcare.
Povera morte sei ramo di sale
grumo di dubbio che non sai
se graziarmi del tempo che rimane.

8/8

death you're a poor thing...

AMELIA ROSSELLI

A poor thing you are death for sure
if you've let me get so close to him
(and therefore to you) while he was dying
if you have scared me so little as to confer
an ounce of sleep close to his pillow.
A poor wee creature you are if from childhood till today
you've made yourself a hedge shaped by clippers:
(now the face of a rooster, now of a dog)
which it takes so little effort to climb over.
Poor death you are a branch of salt
a clot of doubt unsure whether
to grace me with what time remains.

Ritratto di tuffatrice

Charles Darwin annotava quanti pensieri nascano da una testa immersa in acqua fredda.

Affiorando dal mare invernale
valuta il rosso pompeiano delle gambe
il grigio delle labbra
il bianco che riga i polpastrelli
infine il sesso
stretto nel gelo come in vita.

Portrait of a Woman Diving

*Charles Darwin noted how many thoughts form in a head
immersed in cold water.*

Emerging from the winter sea
she considers her legs' Pompeian madder
the grey of her lips
the puckered fingertips
even the sex
cased in ice as it is in life.

Acquedotto

Mi sveglio presto per vedere
un acquedotto lungo come un treno
tra i pini, le nuvole,
un grumo di pecore e di prati.

In treno penso alla pietra sollevata, fermata da una spinta
calcolata, eretta da schiavi, mantenuta da schiavi (come ora)
vedo l'inclinarsi dell'acqua (viene dalle comete)
e il suo mai– riposo, il ritmo delle gocce (ancora oggi) fino alle
fontane.

Quando arrivo mi appoggio a un tronco per guardare.
Guardo in alto. Le arcate scorrono nel vuoto.
Se non sentiamo le grida sotto gli archi di trionfo
e aggiungiamo le parole:
arte e architettura e precisiamo: civile,
allora, forse, troviamo un po' pace,
la stessa che danno gli scheletri
composti nei musei.

Aqueduct

Rome. Fine rain. Wind: South-westerly. Intensity: strong breeze.

I wake up early to see
an aqueduct as long as a train
between the pines, the clouds,
clusters of sheep and of fields.

In the train I think of the stone hefted and slotted by a deft
shove, erected by slaves, maintained by slaves (as it still is);
I see the tilt of the water (that comes from comets)
and its ceaseless turmoil, the rhythm of drop
after drop that (still today) reaches the fountains.

When I arrive I lean on a trunk to look.
I look on high. The arcades flow in the void.
If we don't hear the cries under the triumphal arches
and we add the words
art and architecture, and specify civic,
then – just perhaps – we can find peace
of the sort that assails no lulls us seeing
human bones laid out in a museum.

Cucire

Quand'ero piccola, tutte le donne di casa maneggiavano aghi. Mi hanno sempre affascinato gli aghi, hanno un potere magico. L'ago serve a ricucire gli strappi. E' una richiesta di perdono. Non è mai aggressivo, non è uno spillo.

LOUISE BOURGEOIS

Cuci una federa per ogni ricordo, mettili a dormire, dai loro il sonno di un lenzuolo di lino e infilzali sul telo. L'edera rende la notte verde, una mela cade sull'erba ma tu imbastisci e cuci. Servono spilli e aghi. Serve precisione.

Sewing

When I was growing up, all the women in my house were using needles. I have always had a fascination with the needle, the magic power of the needle. The needle is used to repair damage. It's a claim to forgiveness. It is never aggressive – it's not a pin.

LOUISE BOURGEOIS

Sew a pillowcase for every memory, put them to sleep, give them the sleep of a linen sheet and fix them to the material. Ivy turns the night green, an apple falls on the grass but you tack and sew. Which needs pins and needles. Needs precision

*   *   *

Un giorno ho pensato che ci sarebbe voluto tempo, proprio quando mancava il tempo, per cucire lentamente vicino a una finestra.

Quello che avevo scritto poteva stare in un lenzuolo. Poesie, foto, qualche pensiero. Immagino chi ha inventato l'ago. Era vicino al fuoco e di colpo ha visto che l'osso più affilato (come la spina) teneva insieme la pelle. Spina e pelle. Osso. Quello che la morte smembrava poteva essere unito di nuovo.

Da piccola cucivo foglie di castagno tra loro fino a farne corone. Sognavo di fare vestiti completamente verdi appena rigati di nero dalle spine dei ricci. Sopportavo che mi entrassero nelle mani. Le corone erano perfette, ma fragili. Bastava una folata di vento e si decomponevano volando a caso nel castagneto.

*   *   *

One day I thought that there would still be time, just when there wasn't any, slowly to sew beside the window.

What I had written could be fixed on bed linen. Poems, photos, some thoughts. I imagine the one who invented the needle. He was beside the fire and suddenly saw that the sharpest bone (like a thorn) still held onto some hair. Thorn and hair. Bone. What death had put asunder could be joined again.

When I was young I sewed chestnut leaves together to make a crown. I dreamed of making clothes that were completely green but faintly lined with the black of sea-urchin spines. I could put up with them entering my hands. The crowns were perfect, but fragile. Just a gust of wind and they scattered flying wherever in the chestnut wood.

*   *   *

Se devo scrivere poesie ora che invecchio
voglio vederle scorrere, perdersi in altri corpi
prendere vita e nel frattempo splendere sulle cose vicine,
tenermi compagnia come le cipolle sbucciate nella luce
mentre preparo un brodo con gli occhiali offuscati
appunto un verso su un foglio e a volte mi ferisco
scambiando la penna col coltello.

*　*　*

If I have to write poems now I'm growing old
I'd like to see them flow away, lose themselves
in other bodies, come alive and at the same time
shine on things to hand, keep me company
like onions peeled in the light
as I prepare a soup with steamed-up specs
and jot down a verse on a page, and sometimes
cut myself, mistaking the pen for the knife.

*   *   *

> *... the years, the years.*
> *Down their carved names the raindrop ploughs.*

THOMAS HARDY

Non riesco a sentirti, sta passando un camion carico di ferro, ogni parola spenta dalle sbarre di ferro, ogni nome folgorato dal clangore del ferro, lucido e nero di pioggia senza passato o futuro. Il desiderio non è più l'affamato che guarda dalla finestra la casa illuminata.

*   *   *

… the years, the years.
Down their carved names the raindrop ploughs.

THOMAS HARDY

I can't hear you – a lorry laden with iron
is trundling past, and every word's drowned out
by the iron bars, every name erased
by the foundry thunder and clangour
of iron, shiny and black under a rain
without past, without future.
Desire's no longer the hungry creature
who peers through glass at the palace of light.

Spettri

Sostentati dal nulla
esistenti solo dove si sogna
fluttuanti senza sapere
non più concreti del vapore
che sale dalla teiera
eppure ancora capaci di sentire
la forma di ogni separazione
la precisione con cui la morte
ci tagliava via uno dall'altro:
lo spazio che faceva esponendoci
vuoti di luce, poi sfaldati.

Ghosts

Sustained by nothing, only
existing where we are dreamt,
wavering without sensation,
no more substantial than
steam from a teapot yet
still able to feel the shape
of every separation,
the exactness with which
death has severed us
from each other, the space
it left that reveals us
emptied of light, then crumbling.

Mattino 7:00–12:00

coperto

Maestrale

(voci sovrapposte)

All' alba siamo coraggiosi.
La musica della sveglia ci sorprende.
La *Ciaccona* di Bach alla radio ci controlla
annuncia tra le lancette: vivrete.
Siamo vissuti, stiamo ancora vivendo.
Quante ore, l'intero giorno?
Bisogna rendere onore a tutto questo:
coprire le spalle, circondare il collo.
Metterò un golf, la sciarpa, stringerò il bavero al capotto.
La luce cade nelle tazze, dondola sul latte.
Siamo sopravvissuti almeno per sederci in cucina
le mani sul tavolo, le teste in fiamme
sotto due lampade dai paralumi
a quadri bianchi e rossi, rossi.

Morning 7.00–12.00

overcast

mistral

(superimposed voices)

At dawn we are full of courage.
The alarm clock's music takes us by surprise.
Bach's *Chaconne* on the radio governs our mood
and says between the dials: you'll live.
We have lived, we're still alive.
For many hours, for the whole day?
We need to pay tribute to all of this:
to cover our shoulders, wrap up our necks.
Put sweaters on, scarves, turn up our coat collars.
Light falls on the cups, sways over the milk.
We have at least survived to sit in the kitchen,
hands on the table, heads in flames
under two lamps whose shades
checkered with white and red, and red.

* * *

Non ti ho detto che la mia paura è una piccola macchia:
una zona calva, una frazione di pelle nuda.
Vedevo il suo impercettibile ingrigirsi.
La paura s'imperla come un' ostrica
il bordo sfrangiato di grigio piùscuro.
Tanto piccola da non essere spiegabile.
Screpolata, Tanto insignificante
da non darmi voce per gridare la scoperta
che il male non si espande ma si addensa.

*   *   *

I didn't tell you my fear is a small stain,
a bald patch, a speck of naked skin.
I saw its imperceptible greying.
Fear fashions a pearl as does an oyster,
its edge lustrous with a darker grey.
So small as to remain untold and unexplained.
Scraped. So insignificant, it makes the voice mute
that would have cried out at discovering
evil doesn't spread, just grows more dense.

Lezione

Oggi guardando la città al mattino e i palazzi tremanti di vapore
ho pensato al Giappone, alla casa di Basho
vista l'anno scorso ad aprile
alle sue mappe con le descrizioni dei luoghi
al suo cappello di canne dentro una bacheca.
Nel cortile minuscolo con il banano da cui prende il nome
c'è una rana di pietra – uno stagno –
un suono di acqua mossa che ricorda i suoi versi.
Tutto era breve dal tetto alla fontana fino alla stanza
dove le sue poesie stanno modestamente in mezzo a quelle di altri
senza nessun rilievo tranne quel soprannome: basho.

Allora non sapevo, non sapeva il custode,
né i vecchi poeti raccolti nel giardino
quanto si accatastava sul destino
nessuno in quel momento ricordava
quanti diversi tipi di tremore siamo costretti a imparare.

Lesson

Today watching the city and its tower blocks trembling with heat
I thought of Japan, of Basho's house
seen last April,
of his maps with descriptions of places,
of his straw hat hung inside a glass case.
In the tiny courtyard with the banana tree from which
he took his name there was a stone frog – a small pool –
a sound of moving water which recalls his lines.
Everything was foreshortened from the fountain to the room
where his poems are modestly displayed alongside others'
without distinction but for that surname: basho.

I didn't know then, nor did the attendant
nor the old poets gathered in the garden
the weight of the pile that fate was stacking up –
none of us remembered how many
different kinds of tremor we are forced to learn.

*   *   *

Lo spirito – dice Eckhart – è una montagna di piombo incurante
del vento leggero. Amo quel vento. Non sono quella montagna.
Improvvisamente verso sera il pensiero si schiarisce.
Non piombo ma aria sul fiume.
Le pietre trasparenti, una luce che rallenta e cura.
Un sollievo venuto da non so dove ma reale.
Un fruscio, uno stormire di foglie, sì la memoria che scroscia
copre i ricordi, confonde i visi e i gesti, finalmente.

*   *   *

The spirit – according to Eckhart – is a mountain of lead unaware
      of the light wind.
I love that wind. I'm not that mountain. Suddenly towards evening
      thought clarifies.
Not lead but air over the river.
Transparent stones, light that slackens its pace and heals.
Relief that arrives from nowhere but is real.
A stirring, a rustle of leaves, yes memory's drenching cloudburst
covers all tracks, confuses faces, gestures – finally.

ACKNOWLEDGEMENTS

The poems in this selection are drawn from the following five Italian collections by Antonella Anedda: *Residenze invernali* (Winter Residences), Crocetti, 1992; *Notti di pace occidentale* (Nights of Western Peace), Donzelli, 1999; *Il catalogo della gioia* (Catalogue of Joy), Mondadori, 2003; *Dal balcone del corpo* (From the Body's Balcony), Mondadori, 2007; and *Salva con nome* (Save As), Mondadori, 2012; and from the prose work *La vita dei dettagli* (The Life of Details), Donzelli, 2009;

Acknowledgements are due to the editors of the following publications where some of these translations first appeared: *The American Reader, Bengal Lights, Il Porto di Toledo, Modern Poetry in Translation, The New Republic, Oxford Poetry, Poem, Poetry Review, Qualm, The Stinging Fly, The Times Literary Supplement,* and *World Literature Today*. Some of these translations have appeared in the following anthologies: *The Faber Book of Italian 20th-Century Poems,* ed. Jamie McKendrick (Faber, 2004); *New European Poets,* ed. Wayne Miller and Kevin Prufer (Graywolf, 2008); *The FSG Book of Twentieth-Century Italian Poetry,* ed. Geoffrey Brock (Farrar, Straus and Giroux, 2012), and *Contemporary Italian Poetry,* ed. Pietro Montorfano (University of New York State/Gradiva, 2014).

This book has been selected to receive financial assistance from English PEN's 'PEN Translates!' programme, supported by Arts Council England. English PEN exists to promote literature and our understanding of it, to uphold writers' freedoms around the world, to campaign against the persecution and imprisonment of writers for stating their views, and to promote the friendly co-operation of writers and the free exchange of ideas. www.englishpen.org